THE
HUMAN MACHINE

SECRETS OF SUCCESS

BY

E. R. THOMPSON, M.A.

FOREWORD

BY

M. J. PENNY

Contents

Foreword by M. J. Penny	
Foreword by E. R. Thompson	9
HOW TO THINK	10
HOW TO GET UP	11
BE PUNCTUAL!	12
DON'T WORRY!	13
THE DRILL SERGEANT	14
DOING NOTHING	15
BE INTERESTED!	16
OILED WHEELS	17
A WILLING SERVANT	18
WASTED POWER	19
HOW TO CONCENTRATE (1)	20
HOW TO CONCENTRATE (2)	21
HOW TO CONCENTRATE (3)	22
HOW TO CONCENTRATE (4)	23
THINKING SUCCESS	24
LADDER BUILDING	25
CONQUERING SHYNESS	26
KIM'S GAME	27
LEARNING TO OBSERVE	28
A MEMORY SECRET	29
CLEARING THE GROUND	30
THE FIRST RULE	31
THE WILL TO LEARN	32
USE YOUR IMAGERY	33
NAMES AND FACES	34
LEARNING POETRY	35
OUR MEMORY GAME	36
A FEW RULES	37
CURING THE BLUES	38
THOSE NERVES	39
THINK STRAIGHT	40
HOW TO MAKE MONEY	41
THE HOLIDAY MIND	42

CHARACTER BUILDING	43
HUMAN DONKEYS	44
THE POWER-HOUSE	45
EYES FRONT!	46
EXERCISING THE WILL	47
THE CONCRETE PROBLEM	48
THE CROSS-ROADS	49
MEN AS GODS	50
FALSE PRIDE	51
THE UPHILL ROAD	52
THE LIGHTED WAY	53
DAY DREAMS	54
ON GUARD!	55
DANGER!	56
LOOK OUTWARDS	57
AMOEBA-MEN	58
THE PHYSICAL BASE	59
FEAR	60
COURAGE	61
FACING FEAR	62
COURAGE AND FEAR	63
THE OPEN DOOR	64
HOLDING YOUR OWN	65
SELF-REALISATION	66
SELF-DEVELOPMENT	67
NEVER SAY DIE!	68
SEEK YOUR SELF!	69
WELL-FITTING TIGHTS	70
FIGHTING TO WIN	71
LEADERS TO NOWHERE	72
AUTOMATIC MACHINERY	73
PLAYTIME	74
THINK FIRST	75
THAT TIRED FEELING!	76
THINK FOR YOURSELF!	77
BEING ORIGINAL	78

BRAINS AND BUMPS	79
TREMENDOUS TRIFLES	80
DANGEROUS DETAILS	81
MINDS AND MOBS	82
TENNIS TIPS	83
THE LIVING MECHANISM	84
COMMON SENSE	85
ROSE TINTS	86
MORAL COURAGE	87
MENTAL REVOLT	88
GENERAL INTELLIGENCE	89

Foreword
by
M. J. Penny

"The Universe is change; our life is what our thoughts make it"
Marcus Aurelius (121-180AD)

If you take a look through any bookstore, chances are you will find a multitude of books taking pride of place amid the self-help section.

The popular genre surrounding self-help, is however not a recent thing. Positive psychology has been developing for hundreds of years and the search for such Truth began thousands of years ago. Aristotle (384-322 BC) stated 'Happiness is the meaning and the purpose of life, the whole aim and end of human existence'.

British philosophical writer, James Allen (1864-1912) pointed towards positive psychology in his 1903 publication 'As a Man Thinketh' in which he sums up human existence by revealing that thoughts precede actions. Therefore what we think about the most becomes reflected physically as our reality.

Along with Allen, further philosophical writers such as William Atkinson (1862-1932), Robert Collier (1885-1950), Thomas Carlyle (1795-1881) and Ralph Waldo Emerson (1802-1883) to name just some of the figures central to the 'New Thought' movement of their day, further theories supporting their ideals were reinforced by eminent psychologists in the field.

Such ideals purported that each man and woman were responsible for their own happiness. They need only recognise the power that was dormant within them and through mastering their own thoughts; they could decide for themselves how any situation would affect them.

Suggesting that society was still in its infancy, men and

woman need only assert will-power to gain mastery over their thoughts and minds. Lofty ideals such as these expressed in an era when religion was dominant was not taken well by the Church, resulting in the prohibition of particular 'New Thought' books.

Further breakthroughs in psychology continued to suggest that patients embracing the power of positive thought recovered faster than their non-practising peers. It was found that the relationship between the conscious and the subconscious mind was the cornerstone that determined the actions and emotional mindset of an individual in any given situation.

> *"We are what we repeatedly do. Excellence therefore is not an act but a habit"*
> Aristotle

The following book began as weekly articles in the UK magazine 'John Bull'. The magazine which is reported to have a circulation of 1,350,000 became Britain's best selling magazine throughout the early 20th century, and in later years featured fiction from the popular writers of the day, such as Agatha Christie and J. B. Priestly.

Edward Roffe Thompson was a journalist and then later became Editor of the magazine. His articles were embraced by thousands as he inspired a nation, teaching them common-sense wisdom. Born in 1893, the son of a musician, E. R. Thompson received such momentous praise for his articles that he was urged by his readers to publish them in book form.

His ability to capture the imagination of the UK public through his instruction to recondition the mind and form new habits of thinking was bold for the day and supported the non-conformist air of the magazine.

In 1925, his book 'The Human Machine' was first published. It was an important year for Thompson as his marriage to celebrated film critic and journalist Caroline Lejeune took place in June in Chelsea.

As he reassured readers back then, guiding them through the troubles of everyday life, the following articles as written by E. R. Thompson are provided in hope that they reassure readers today.

TO

MY MOTHER

WHOSE UNSWERVING FAITH IN THIS
PARTICULAR HUMAN MACHINE
HAS BEEN THE GREATEST SECRET OF ITS
SUCCESS

{By E. R. Thompson}

FOREWORD
by
E. R. Thompson

These little articles, which originally appeared in the pages of John Bull, are reprinted in response to a widespread demand for their collection into book form.

They contain little that is original, for the common-sense side of psychology is the possession of all who read and think about what they read.

If in the future, as they have done in the past, they help a single individual to make the best use of the marvellous machine that we call the mind; their object will have been achieved.

The possibilities inherent in the Human Machine are infinite. The most these articles can claim is to be regarded as signposts to the borderland of a country that is, at present, largely unexplored.

E. R. Thompson.

93 Long Acre
London.

Learn To Think

One of the greatest, if not the greatest, forces governing the human body is habit. From getting up in the morning to lying down at night, nine-tenths of our actions are automatic.

With most people, far too few actions are made into habits, with the result that they spend a good part of each day deciding or regretting things that ought hardly be conscious at all.

The result is that mental energy is being used up for trivial daily duties that should be free for other and more important things. A man with an indecisive mind is simply a man who has not troubled to form enough habits to set his mind free for higher work.

Such a man is the most miserable creature on earth, for he allows his nervous system to be his enemy, instead of making it his ally. On the mental side, habit is just as important. No one who has a brain inside his head can help thinking, of course, in the broad sense of the word.

But to think in an active sense-to use the brain as a sort of dynamo for the manufacture of originality, of thought FORCE, is more rare.

Yet everyone can do it if conscious effort is used, if effort is made every day, if, in other words, a HABIT of thought is formed. The man who can think is always master of the man who can only do. The men who rise highest in this world are those who can both think and do.

It is never too late to form habits. The older one gets, the more difficult it is, that is all. Those who give the habit of thought a little daily practice are those who will sooner or later be rewarded by a world that has no use for indecision and mere drift.

How to Get Up

Getting up in the morning is a little winter-time problem that affects us all.

The amount of nervous energy we expand in coming to the point is out of all proportion to the nature of the task.

Make getting up a habit, and it will cease to be a problem. Viewed coldly, it is just as easy to get up as to stay in bed. It is simply a question of making a decision and acting on it. It is a question of willpower. A person who cannot act on a decision has weak will: and his problem is to educate it and make it strong.

If you find it difficult to get up in the morning, tell yourself the night before that you CAN. It helps to say it aloud. Say it firmly. Say it as though you mean it. It is no use being half-hearted about it.

You are giving orders to your subconscious self. If it is done properly you will find on waking that the decision is uppermost in your mind. Then comes the crucial moment. If you stop to think you are lost. Let your subconscious mind impel your muscles to action before reasoning powers gain the upper hand!

Every night, just before you go to sleep, tell yourself that you CAN get up. Never miss a night. Each morning you succeed will make next morning's task easier. Each morning you give way will make it harder.

The nervous system does not readily forgive weakness. Steady practice, night and morning, backed by real effort, will establish the getting-up HABIT.

When that is done, the problem is solved.

Be Punctual!

One of the great truths of psychology is that thoughts tend to become actions.

If a person persists in thinking he is ill, he will most certainly become ill, although really there is nothing whatever the matter with him. The extent to which the mind can limit the body is almost without limit.

Thought developed along the right lines can even cure you of such a bad habit as unpunctuality. If you are one of those people who find they simply cannot get to work on time, just sit down and think about it. You will quickly realise that you are unpunctual because you have not a clear sense of duty.

You see no reason for being punctual. Really you have a double duty – to your own self-respect and to your employer. Once you have set your mind towards the goal of duty, the battle is half won.

Unpunctuality is largely due to a policy of drift. A sense of duty means having a purpose in view. In this case it means being fair to your employer and to yourself. Get your purpose clearly fixed, and before you know it you will be making the little details of your life fit into the scheme.

You will be making a point of getting up half an hour earlier for your bus or train. You will begin to organise your life. You will cease to be a drifter. Lack of organisation is the cause of unpunctuality.

The man who cannot be bothered to organise his life has an untidy mind. The result is he leads and untidy life. He is respected by no one-not even himself.

Don't Worry!

Worry is a demon that can make the whole world look black. Brooding in secret warps and twists the mind, and makes misery for everyone concerned. It is worthwhile, next time you are irritable and venting your anger on everyone with whom you come into contact, to sit down quietly and think about it.

Make sure that what you allege to be the grievance is the real cause of your anger. It is one of the peculiarities of the human mind that an unpleasant thought tends to sink down and be "forgotten." We don't like to be continually reminded of unpleasant things. But buried deep in the mind, the unpleasant thought is busy generating energy. This energy attaches itself to other thoughts, and we become morose for no apparent cause.

We get angry with those around us for the most trivial reasons. We are angry, as it were, by a mistake. Therefore sit down and think. Soon, you will be quite sure of the real source of your irritation. When you have found it, stop bottling it up. Talk about it. Talk about it to your husband, to your wife, to your friend. Never mind who it is. So long as they will listen to you TALK about it.

By talking about it you set free the energy that is being repressed and crushed down. The unpleasant idea that is worrying you will be destroyed. It will cease to colour your thoughts and actions, and you will speedily feel a different person. You will cease to be a nuisance to yourself and everyone around you.

The sensible man broods about nothing. When he feels miserable he talks about it-and feels better.

The Drill Sergeant

Do we cry because we feel sad, or do we feel sad because we cry? Do we run away because we feel frightened, or are we frightened because we run away? These are not such silly questions as they sound. A great deal depends upon whether the bodily action or the emotion comes first. The growing opinion of psychologists is that in a great many cases the bodily action does come first.

This can easily be proved. Kneel down, put your hands together, close your eyes – and you will quickly feel a religious feeling creeping over you. Your bodily attitude has called forth the appropriate emotion.

This leads to very important conclusions. It means that, just as mind can control and affect the body, so the body can have a direct influence on the mind. It follows that if you are feeling depressed the worst possible thing is to sit hunched up in a chair holding your head in your hands.

The physical attitude of depression only brings out the mental side more strongly. The thing to do is smile, to straighten your back, square your shoulders, and get busy with some cheerful occupation.

Chop some wood, break some coal, go for a brisk walk. And whatever you do, do it with a will. Do it with the corners of your mouth turned up. Do it without a wrinkle on your brow. Whistle about it. Sing about it.

Your mind will quickly follow your body and a cheerful emotion takes the place of your black mood. Now you know how mind and body can react on each other, use your knowledge. When your mind is depressed make your body order it to be cheerful. It will readily obey.

Doing Nothing

Leisure is necessary for everyone. The man who uses his brain, the woman who runs a home, all need the rest. There is a difference, however, between rest and idleness.

Time is the most precious commodity in the world. Not a minute should be wasted. "Doing nothing" should be regarded as a relative term. More rest can often be got out of a change of occupation than out of idleness.

So called "rest" is often an excuse for mere laziness. Some people sit and think. Others just sit!

Those who just sit are always the most miserable people on earth. There sitting always ends in their brooding over petty grievances and fancied wrongs. Day in and day out the human machine generates energy. If this energy is not utilised trouble results.

The best rest for a manual worker is brain activity – such as reading. The man who uses his brain all day will find real relaxation in some work that needs the use of muscle – gardening, carpentry and so forth.

Nevertheless, everybody benefits occasionally by real idleness, when, for half an hour or so, they literally do nothing. The danger is lest such idleness becomes a master. Use it sparingly as a means to an end. But use your spare time wisely. The happy man is he who is using his flow of nervous energy in creation of some sort.

Complete idleness is a medicine, and medicines are not necessary healthy.

Be Interested!

There is a vast reservoir of energy locked up inside the human machine, waiting to be tapped by those who know how. While Nature has given everyone an equipment of capacities, and possibilities for thought and action, these are as useless as a machine deprived of motive power unless they are nursed and provided with exercise.

What happens to a man is frequently of more importance than what is born in him. Human tendencies are like tender plants. Starve them, and they will wither and die; feed them, and they will eventually grow into sturdy trees. That is why everybody should have a hobby. A Golden Rule in life is "Be interested!"

No matter what it is, be interested in **SOMETHING**.

Many a man who feels his ability lies in mechanical things, for instance, finds himself changed to an office desk.

If he has no outlet for his suppressed store of energy his work will be drudgery.

It will make him physically and mentally tired. He will be discontented and bitter. If such a man has a hobby that will give his mechanical inclinations exercise and outlet, his daily work will cease to be a laborious task.

By unlocking one store of nervous energy he releases others. His mental outlook will be forward and optimistic, instead of pessimistic and backwards.

Hobbies may be more than pleasant recreations. They may be made the solid background of life. Many great men were born-true: more were made: still more made themselves.

Have a hobby. Be interested. Give your latent powers a chance to develop.

Oiled Wheels

To say of a man that "he takes the line of least resistance" is held to imply a serious reproach.

True, used in a certain sense, the phrase does mean that such a man is lacking in moral calibre, unable to fight temptation, drifting aimlessly wherever the tides of life carry him.

All the same, one of our most pressing problems is so to think and act that the human machine runs with as little effort and strain as possible. Work is not unpleasant. It is when the work involves strain that it becomes labour.

For the most part we become weary, irritable, and worn-out, not because of what we do, but because of what we do not do.

"Whatsoever thy hand findeth to do, do it with thy might," is ancient advice, but it contains a profound psychological truth.

The man who is absorbed heart and soul in his work during the day finds the work flow easily; he goes home tired maybe, but with a reserve of nervous energy, ready for his hobbies and his pleasures.

The man who has to be continually stifling thoughts of things outside his work, killing desires to be else-where, and side- stepping wishes for unobtainable pleasures, goes home with frayed nerves, physically and mentally exhausted.

The energy that should have been driving the machine smoothly along the paths of well-ordered work has been dissipated in fighting useless battles. He has no reserves left.

The line of least resistance in work **PAYS**. It can be attained by concentrating on the job in hand and refusing to be led aside by irrelevant details. The discontented worker is a mental martyr, and voluntary martyrdom is never a paying game.

A Willing Servant

[1]M. Coue has achieved fame through his belief in the health- giving effects of saying to oneself, "Each day, in every way, I get better and better." He is preaching a great truth. The mind has a direct effect on the body, particularly the subconscious mind. A man's mind may be made either his willing slave or his merciless tyrant. Sleeplessness is a far too prevalent affliction nowadays. If you suffer from insomnia, tackle it now. There is a better method than counting sheep. Make use of the powers of your subconscious mind. See that your sleeping attitude is right. See that your muscles are completely relaxed. See above all, that fresh air can get into the room. Now see that your mental attitude is right. Say: "I CAN go to sleep. Of course I can go asleep." Say it with conviction, and when you say it, mean it. After a little time say: "Now I am getting sleepy. I feel tired. I am not able to keep my eyelids open." And when you say it mean it. Now say: "I am going to sleep." Say it about twenty times. And when you say it, BELIEVE it. Follow this up by about twenty slow, deep breaths. Ten minutes of this and you should be asleep. Perhaps the first time you will not succeed. Never mind. Do it the next night; and keep on until you do succeed. In the end your subconscious mind will believe that when you say you are going to sleep you are earnest, and it will help you. But if you don't firmly believe it yourself you will get no assistance from your subconsciousness.

It will readily obey orders, but it will never aid hypocrisy.

---

[1] Émile Coué – French psychologist (1857-1926). Identified and introduced the method of Autosuggestion. The Coué method involved repetitious thought centred on an optimistic outlook and state of mind to supplement conventional medicine to patients. He believed that by adopting a positive mental state, patients recovered faster.

Wasted Power

Last week I stressed the necessity for concentration if work is to be accomplished without undue wear and tear. Many people, however, fall into the error of making concentration an end in itself, instead of merely a means to an end – the smooth accomplishment of a given task.

Watch an expert and an inexpert worker attempting the same job. The former concentrates on his work, but works with an effortless ease that hides the painstaking care given to every detail. The latter is also concentrating – to a degree painful to watch. But he is concentrating on his efforts to concentrate. He is engaged in an intense fight – with himself. When he is finished he feels proud of the effort he has made, and he makes the mistake of measuring results by his feelings, instead of the amount he has accomplished. In reality there has been as much waste of power as though a [2]Nasmyth hammer had been used to crack a nut. Nothing could be more fallacious than the idea that the harder we make the task the better we shall do it. The aim of every worker should be to do the maximum of work with the minimum display of effort. It is always the expert worker who makes the least fuss about it. We come back to the whole question of Habit. When attention becomes a habit, so soon is the brain freed from the effort to concentrate and able to devote itself to the work. Remember that, other things being equal, the more easily you work the more you will accomplish.

Rightly used, concentration is the oil that makes the wheels go round. Wrongly used, it is merely grit that stops them moving at all.

---

[2] The Nasmyth Hammer – a power hammer driven by steam patented in 1842 by James Hall Nasmyth (1808-1890). Used to shape forgings for machines in industry. Varying in weight, ranging from 45 kilograms to 90 metric tons, the hammer was used to forge the paddle shaft of the SS Great Britain, but could also break an egg placed in a wineglass without shattering or breaking the glass itself.

How to Concentrate (1)

We have seen the importance of concentration to secure smooth and efficient work. Let us now see how to bring this state of mind about.

The root of the whole matter is interest. Concentration merely means the power of giving undivided attention to something. Where we are interested in that something, this close attention follows automatically.

There is no such thing as inattention. A man who is not attending to the work he is supposed to be doing is not in a state of attending to nothing. He is actively attending to something else outside his work.

The trouble is that his work does not interest him his mind wanders off it to something that does interest him.

If you who read this are a young man searching for a career, make certain that your choice falls on something that interests you. Be sure that you will never make a success of work that fails to rouse your interest. You will not be able to give it enough attention.

If you are already tied to work that is uninteresting — what then? Make it interesting! There is no job in the world that has not got its interesting side if you look for it hard enough. Take a pride in your work. Set for yourself a standard. Criticise yourself.

Above all take a fresh viewpoint. If you really search for the interesting side of a job you will be astonished to find how quickly you will find it. And once you have created some interest you will automatically begin to attend.

You will begin, in other words, to concentrate. When you do that you will be well on the road to becoming an expert.

How to Concentrate (2)

WE saw last week that the creation of interest is the essential starting-point for concentration. Concentration—or paying attention—is an ability that can be cultivated to any extent. In other words, it can be made into a habit.

Like any other habit, it needs constant practice if success is to be attained. Here is a simple way of giving the habit of paying close attention the daily practice that is needed to establish it firmly.

Everybody can manage to find a spare half-hour for reading. Use this as your practice ground. Forget about that enthralling novel you wish to read. You can find another odd half-hour in which to enjoy that.

Reading novels involves no effort anyway. It is interesting, and automatically holds your attention. Choose instead some book in which you are not interested. Take, for example, a solid book on economics, history, politics.

For half an hour a day force yourself to read it, and force yourself to follow its arguments. Bring your will-power into play, and hold your attention to its task in spite of all temptations to the contrary.

It will not be easy—at first. Habit formation is never easy in its initial stages. Make a rule never to miss a single day. And having made the rule—stick to it. Gradually you will find your self-appointed task growing easier.

And there will come a day when you will find it needs no effort at all. For your constant attention to your subject will have brought an unexpected reward. You will find yourself interested in it.

Having become interested, you will need no further spur. And, incidentally, you will have substantially increased your knowledge.

How to Concentrate (3)

The man who is master of his mind can direct his forces at will in whatever direction he desires. He needs no guidance in what to do and what not to do.

The man who is learning how to direct and control the immense powers within him often fails because he takes too much for granted.

Last week I outlined a simple exercise in concentration. There are many little aids to success that must not be overlooked. Remember, you are attempting to form a Habit. See to it that you give yourself every chance.

Don't begin reading that book, for instance, while you are still tired from your day's work. Wait a little, until both body and brain have recovered from the strain. Otherwise you start under a heavy handicap.

See to it that, so far as possible, your surroundings are a help and not a hindrance. Choose a quiet place where you will be reasonably free from interruption. Later, none of these details will matter much: in the beginning their importance cannot be too strongly emphasised.

Don't even neglect your bodily attitude. Be comfortable, and see that you have a good light. Your task, in its early stages, will be hard enough without adding to it any physical distractions that can be avoided. And, as far as possible, see that your mind is free from care and worry before you begin.

Your great aim must be to make your nervous system your ally instead of your enemy. Therefore make it as easy and pleasant for it as you can. If you begin by deliberately shutting out all distractions, you will end by not caring whether they exist or not.

For, from another viewpoint, concentration is the ability to ignore everything but work in hand.

How to Concentrate (4)

Several readers have written to ask what is the use of learning to concentrate. On its lowest level the answer is that the man who has so trained his mind that he is able to stick unwaveringly to his work is more commercially valuable than the man who is the victim of the mind-wandering habit.

In this world the big salaries go to the men who are masters of their minds, the men who can direct their brain force in an ordered way. Psychologically the answer is that unless we learn to concentrate we shall be of little use, even to ourselves. Continuous attention to anything is a matter of mental discipline. Except for a few seconds at a time there is no such thing as voluntary attention. Unless we wish to be at the mercy of every passing distraction we must learn how to hold the mind to its task. "The power of applying an attention, steady and undissipated, to a single object, is the sure mark of a superior genius," said [3]Chesterfield.

No doubt in the last resort a genius is born, but I am a firm believer in the theory that a clever man is made, and made very largely by his own endeavours. The man who is aware of the forces that lie within him, and who knows how to make use of them, can do practically anything to which he sets his mind. I leave the subject of concentration by returning again to the question of interest. The richer your mind is in knowledge, in ideas, in original thoughts, the easier you will find concentration. Everything will then suggest some new point, some new angle. The more you know, the more interesting will everything become.

It is the vacant mind that finds it hard to concentrate.

---

[3] The 4th Earl of Chesterfield, (1694-1773). Also known as Lord Chesterfield, born Philip Dormer Stanhope. A Statesman and ambassador at The Hague, Chesterfield wrote more than 400 letters to his son between the years of 1737, imparting his wisdom until his son's death in 1768.

Thinking Success

[4]Virgil, the Roman poet, describing a boat race, says of the winning team: "They can, because they think they can."

Nothing slows up the human machine so much as faint-heartedness. Nothing gives it such an impetus as a supreme belief in one's own abilities. The man who succeeds is he who is firmly persuaded that he can succeed.

The ability to think rightly is a golden key to the door of opportunity. The reason is that we are so made that thoughts always tend to become actions, and actions tend to become habits. If you are not succeeding as you could wish, while someone else is making wonderful progress, the reason is probably not far to seek.

Ten to one you are dominated by a fear that you are not going to succeed. You are deliberately putting on a powerful brake. Ten to one the other man is quite sure he is going to realise his ambition. He is thinking rightly: you are thinking wrongly.

Believe in yourself and in your own powers. Realise that you can, if you think you can. Tell yourself that you can. Think success. Make use of your subconscious self.

Just before you go to sleep, and immediately you wake up, spend a few minutes glorying in your abilities. Unthinking people would call this conceit. The psychologist would call it auto-suggestion. I do not say that you can do anything on earth merely by thinking that you can do it. I do say that such a belief will add fifty per cent to your efficiency.

Why pull against a powerful brake when you can just as easily have a powerful engine to help you along?

---

[4] Quote from Virgil's (70-19 BC) Aeneid

Ladder Building

In spite of innumerable facts to the contrary, mankind clings persistently to the belief that much that happens in our lives is due to chance.

Never was there a greater fallacy. From the beginning of time wise men have insisted that every thought and every act leaves an indelible mark on the character.

"We build the ladder by which we climb," said a great psychologist. "Nothing of good or evil is ever lost: we may forget and forgive, but our nervous system never forgets nor forgives."

It follows that nothing is unimportant. A year hence we shall be what we are because of what we think and do now. It is the present that counts. In physical matters this is easy to see. The man who abuses his body, whether by drugs or any other vicious habit, pays the price.

There is no overdraft possible on the Bank of Nature. This is equally true of mental life. Here, too, Nature is a merciless creditor. The man who scamps his work, who disregards the responsibilities of ordinary life, may think it doesn't matter. But sooner or later the bill will be presented. The carelessness that seems of no account to-day will mean failure when the big responsibility and the big problem have to be faced.

The man who does big things in the world is he who has built the ladder by which he climbed out of faithfulness to the little things and the ordinary things. A man's character is not a matter of chance. He forms it himself—and fashions it as he desires.

Think rightly and you will act rightly. Do the small things well, and the big things will look after themselves.

Conquering Shyness

Many people fail to make much progress in life because they are hampered by self-consciousness. They are shy, tongue-tied, hesitant in speech and action.

They end by lacking confidence in themselves. Often they persuade themselves that they are inferior to those around them. The trouble arises through their thoughts being turned inwards instead of outwards.

The self-conscious man concentrates all his energies on wondering what people are thinking about him. It is a waste of energy, because as a rule they are not thinking about him at all. They haven't time.

The best cure for shyness is (1) to widen your circle of interests; (2) to work towards a definite goal. The more things you are interested in, the more your thoughts will flow outwards and away from unimportant and imagined grievances.

If you have a definite goal in life you will regard as opportunities what you now look upon as ordeals. As a rule the man who is self-conscious is also the man whose life lacks a definite aim. He is drifting, wasting thought-power on self-pity and self-analysis that should be going to force a pathway to success.

Have an aim in life and, what is more, believe in that aim and in your ability to accomplish it. You will soon find yourself too busy looking for ways and means of advancing your ambition to spare any time for useless self-pity.

You will find yourself weighing up and appraising other people—instead of wondering if they are criticising you. To formulate a definite aim in life is to create a source of energy that will sweep away all unhealthy thoughts. The man who sees his goal ahead is not interested in by-paths.

Kim's Game

If you have read [5]Rudyard Kipling's Kim, you will remember that his first training for Secret Service work consisted in his being shown a trayful of little objects, the names of which he had to repeat after looking at them for a few seconds.

He was being taught Observation—the art of using his eyes. Not one person in ten uses his eyes efficiently. That is why so many people complain of having bad memories. Memory does not consist solely in being able to remember. This is only the end of the memory process.

The ease with which you remember depends on how forcibly the idea to be remembered is impressed on your mind to begin with. It is one thing to see—it is quite another to observe. If you look at a thing and merely see it, you get a visual impression that may be anything from a clear picture to a mere vague idea of something familiar to you.

If you both see it and observe it, you will notice details. You will instinctively compare it with other things. You will link it up with other ideas. We shall see later that this is the foundation of good memory.

"Kim's Game" is an excellent way of training your powers of observation. It is worth practising, for unless you observe well you will never remember well. Use your ears as well as your eyes. It is quite possible to be mentally deaf while in possession of two perfectly sound ears.

It is a good plan to play "Kim's Game" blindfolded, using the sense of touch alone. If you want to have a good memory-begin by training your senses.

---

[5] Kim-written by Rudyard Kipling. First published as a serial in McClure's Magazine in 1900. Re-published by Macmillan & Co in 1901.

Learning to Observe

Training the senses to work efficiently, with which I dealt last week, is a matter that must be treated with the utmost seriousness by all who desire a good memory.

If you wish to discover the difference between merely seeing and really observing, try this little exercise. You have seen an ordinary postage stamp hundreds of times. Can you describe such a stamp accurately?

Take a sheet of paper and write down a list of all the details that appear on a postage stamp. When you have put down everything you can remember—and you will be surprised to find how little that is—get another sheet of paper and a postage stamp.

Make another list with the stamp before you. Look at it closely: go over it again and again until you are quite sure you have missed nothing. Now compare your two lists, and you will see what I mean when I say that while we are continually seeing things we rarely observe them.

Here is another excellent way of learning to use your eyes; a little game [6]Charles Dickens was fond of playing. Think of some well-stocked shop-window you will pass on your way home from work. As you pass— without actually stopping—see how many articles you can fix in your memory. As soon as you get home write down all you can remember. Next day, take your list with you and compare it with the window.

At first you will be surprised at the small amount you can remember; but if you practise steadily you will soon be astonished to find how much you can remember with just a glance. As always, it is practice that counts.

---

[6] Charles Dickens – English Victorian writer (1812-1870).

A Memory Secret

When training your senses to function efficiently, don't forget smell, taste, and touch. It is true that civilisation has made it possible to rely less and less on our senses for information, but the more aids to memory, the better that memory is going to be.

Since our knowledge of the world can only reach us via the senses, it is important to see that they are keen. All around us are forces in Nature, a veritable fairyland of colours, sights and sounds, of which our senses give us no knowledge.

They are capable of catching and recording only a small fraction of the messages the outside world is continually sending. What we can do is to see that they catch this small fraction in the most efficient manner.

Let us see where all this leads. Memory depends on what psychologists call the "association of ideas." That is, if two ideas are placed together in the mind they tend to set up a connection between them. In future, whenever we are reminded of one the other tends to be remembered. Try this for yourself. Think of the "Battle of Hastings." Immediately" 1066 "comes to your mind. This is because at school you learned these two ideas together. Now, when you hear the one, up comes the other automatically.

The secret of a good memory is a very simple secret- It is the secret of linking up the fact you wish to remember with as many other facts as you can. But you must make a good start by taking care that the original fact is strongly impressed on your brain.

Keen and efficient senses are the lever that sets the whole memory process in motion.

Clearing the Ground

I have no doubt that if I could have all my readers in front of me and ask them "What sort of a memory have you?" I should get an amazing variety of replies.

They would range all the way from "Excellent" to "Very bad." Some would tell me that they used to have wonderful memories, but that lately they have noticed a sad falling off in efficiency. Yet all the replies would be wrong except "Excellent."

The fact is—and I want to state this as plainly as possible—that if you are in good health you never had a better memory than you have at this moment. Good health, of course, is the first essential. Nothing so quickly lowers the efficiency of the brain as an ailing body.

To those, therefore, who are worried about their memories, I say first of all, "See to it that your bodily health is as good as you can make it." Secondly, get rid of the poor ideas of your own powers that you probably have.

Believe me, there is nothing wrong with your memory. What is wrong is that you learn badly, learn wrongly, or don't know how to set about learning. "Learn better and you will remember better" is the motto with which to guide your efforts.

Cleverness has little or nothing to do with it; mans very clever people complain of having bad memories. So if you have persuaded yourself that your memory is bad, be of good heart. Realise that your memory is all right, and that what you have to do is to learn how to use it to better advantage.

How to do this will be the purpose of future articles.

The First Rule

If you know your [7]Sherlock Holmes you will remember that he was a walking encyclopdia of crime. He had the details of a thousand cases at his finger-ends.

On the other hand, he knew nothing of a score of subjects about which any ordinary man is well informed. There are any number of people like Sherlock Holmes. A man who has a "poor" memory for details of his daily work will often display a phenomenal memory for cricket scores and averages.

A boy may remember nothing of what he is taught, but his memory for the details of his stamp album would almost put Datas to shame. From Sherlock Holmes to the schoolboy the secret is the same.

One and all they remember those things in which they are vitally interested. In a previous article I likened interest to a key that, rightly used, would unlock vast stores of latent energy, make attention and concentration automatic, and render easy the task of habit formation. Interest and good memory are twins.

It is not only easy to remember things in which we are interested: it is remarkably difficult to forget them! If you are pessimistic about your memory, just take stock of what Sherlock Holmes called your "brain-attic."

Somewhere you will find in it a store of facts that will amaze you by their number and persistence. They may concern work, cricket, football, horses, but whatever they concern, you will find that it is there that your interest lies.

I am often inclined to think that the whole secret of a happy and successful life lies in those two words "Be interested." It is certainly the secret of good memory.

---

[7] Sherlock Holmes – Fictional character and super sleuth created by Scottish author, Sir Arthur Conan Doyle (1859-1930). Doyle wrote fifty six short stories featuring the detective and four novels.

The Will to Learn

ONE of the things that makes a study of the mind so fascinating is that its territory is still very largely an unknown country.

Science has established general principles along which the mind works. We know with fair accuracy how various processes—such as memory—take place, upon what factors they depend, and how we may best use our known powers to attain our ends.

But our knowledge of the mind is not comparable to our knowledge of the body. We know fairly exactly the limits of our bodily powers. A trained athlete, for example, can only jump about six feet, or run a hundred yards in about ten seconds.

It is safe to assume that no one will ever clear ten feet, or do the hundred yards in five seconds. But when we come to the mind we know only very vaguely the common everyday limits to its powers. About the limits of its possible powers we know practically nothing at all.

When all the fraud and superstition are eliminated from Spiritualism and psychic investigations, there remains enough scientific knowledge to make us wonder if there are any limits at all. Telepathy, for instance, is a scientifically established fact. Will-power, with which we shall have to deal fully at a later date, seems capable of tapping an inexhaustible supply of energy.

Since the first part of the memory process is the learning of the facts, it is important that the will should be given an impetus and not act as a brake. "The will to learn "is a scientific way of saying, "You never know what you can do till you try."

If you learn with zest and vigour you will remember with ease.

Use Your Imagery

It is most important, if you are to have a good memory, to find out which type of imagery comes most naturally to you, and which is most vivid.

Close your eyes and think of a railway engine. Do you see the engine "in your mind's eye," as we say? Do you actually see a picture of the engine, clear and detailed, as though you were looking at a print?

People who possess the ability to see these vivid mental pictures of the objects they think about are gifted with "visual imagery." Close your eyes again. Think of the rain beating on the window-pane. Can you hear the sound in imagination? Can you reproduce the sound mentally, as vividly as though the rain were actually beating against the window?

If so, you possess what we call "auditory imagery." Try in a similar way if you can reproduce mentally the sensations of touch, taste, and smell. The type of imagery varies with different people. Some visualise; others hear sounds; a large number do both.

It is important to discover which type of imagery you possess. The reason is simple. If you are a visualiser make sure that you see whatever you wish to remember. If it is a name, for instance, write it down. If you find you can reproduce sounds, be sure you hear what you wish to remember.

If, for example, you want to learn a piece of poetry, read it aloud. Remember that the mind is a machine. Learn how it works and then drive it, instead of just letting it run.

Mental imagery can be an enormous help to memory if you use it intelligently.

Names and Faces

How many times a day do I hear the remark, "I simply cannot remember people's faces!" or "I never remember names!"

Let me say at once that if you don't remember a person's name, in nine cases out of ten it is because you have never heard it. It's easy enough to miss a name during a hurried Introduction. We all do it.

If you don't catch the name, ask for it. People don't mind: it's only you who think they do. What they do mind is to find you have forgotten their name next time you meet. You must get a clear and vivid impression if you are to remember later. Then apply last week's lesson. If you visualise, take care to write the name down when you are alone. If you are auditory, repeat it aloud.

The next thing is to connect the name with the face. Think of them both together: try to associate them definitely in your mind. You have learned to use your eyes. Use them intelligently now. Take a mental snapshot of the person. What colour are his eyes? What shape is his face? What colour is the hair?

All these details are pegs on which to hang the memory: they help to ensure that when next you see the face you will instantly recall the name. The chief function of this close observation is to compel attention. That to which you really attend you will find remarkably difficult to forget.

I don't believe very much in that "bad memory for names and faces." It is usually a matter of carelessness and inattention.

At any rate, it can quickly be made a good memory with intelligent practice.

Learning Poetry

Everyone at some time or other wishes to learn poems off by heart. Beautiful pieces of prose, too, are an excellent addition to one's memories.

There is a right way of learning such extracts in order to recall them easily. Psychologists have done a great deal of experimental work on memory, and they have found that a piece of poetry can be learned most easily if it is read through as a whole, instead of in bits.

The usual—and wrong—way is to read a few lines until they can be remembered, then a few more lines, and so on. Finally, after much labour, the whole poem can be remembered. To do this is to give yourself a great deal of unnecessary work. You form numerous associations between the ends and beginnings of lines where no associations should be.

These false associations tend later to block the memory. This is why so many people can repeat a poem up to a certain point, and then their mind becomes a blank.

The proper way is to read the poem straight through from beginning to end. Then do it again. And again. And yet again. And each time go straight through from beginning to end. There will come a moment when you find you can repeat the poem by heart. You will have learned it almost without knowing it.

This, of course, applies to reasonably short poems of, say, five to ten verses. Supposing you wish to learn a much longer poem? Clearly the thing to do is to divide it into several shorter pieces and follow the same procedure with each.

Try both ways for yourself. The results will interest you.

Our Memory Game

Here is one of the finest memory exercises ever invented.

Take two packs of ordinary playing cards and shuffle them. Spread them face downwards on the table. Let us assume there are three players, A, B, and C. A turns up any two cards he pleases. If these are a "pair"—i.e. two kings, two twos, two fives (of any suit)—A takes them and turns up two more cards.

If the two cards are not a "pair," A turns them face downwards again, taking care not to disturb their position, and B turns up two cards.

Suppose A turned up a king and a two. B turns up a knave and a two. If he can remember the position of A's two he turns it up. If he is correct he takes the pair. He may then turn up another card.

As soon as B breaks down and has turned his cards face downwards again, C turns up two cards and the game proceeds as before. A player may go on collecting "pairs" to any number. His turn does not finish until he fails to turn up corresponding cards.

It will be seen that, before long, success at this game depends on the sheer ability to remember the positions and names of the cards that other players have turned up.

There is no other way of playing the game. If you cannot remember what cards have been turned up and where they lie, you will not win. Absolute concentration is necessary, too. Let your mind wander for a moment and you are lost.

If you think you have a bad memory, play this game a few times. You will probably revise your opinion.

A Few Rules

Let us sum up some of the conclusions to be drawn from our study of memory up to date.

To remember a fact, it must be strongly impressed on the mind. Interest in the learning, and intense concentration on the task, are the main factors.

Never give way to the idea that your memory is poor. Tell yourself firmly that you have a good memory. Remember that this "auto-suggestion," as it is called, has a powerful effect. What is more, you will be telling yourself nothing less than the truth.

Trust your memory. Assuming that the learning has been well done, when you attempt to recall it, what comes strongly to the mind is almost sure to be correct. Just "let it come." This is a case where, nine times out of ten, first thoughts are best.

Remembering depends on the association of ideas. When learning, therefore, put together those things you wish to remember. The more two things are associated, the more will the thought of one tend to call up the other.

Thought is a habit. Train yourself to think logically. Don't wander aimlessly, either in thought or speech. It all helps. Remember that sound health is the physical basis of good memory. Plenty of exercise and fresh air are essential to an alert mind.

Lastly, take a wide interest in people and things. Anything, so long as it is linked up with your thoughts, is a possible aid to memory. Once again, be interested.

Curing the Blues

I have no doubt that all my readers from time to time get the "blues." They come to everybody.

It is usually difficult to say what is wrong. We feel heavy and depressed, life looks black, and sometimes it seems as if it were hardly worth living. The "blues" is a nasty, irritating complaint.

But there is a cure for it as there is for most ailments. In nine cases out of ten such depression is the result of too much thought on one subject, usually a problem or a difficulty that refuses to be solved.

Even the healthiest person is liable to this mental sickness, when the brain goes dizzily round and round a stubborn problem, getting no nearer to a way out. And as mental states are quickly reflected in bodily feelings, we usually end up by feeling tired and listless.

Doctors are fond of recommending a change for bodily ills. Try a complete mental change for mental ills. When you get the "blues" don't go on thinking. Switch your mind to something else; and the more cheerful and different it is the better.

Go out and play a hard game of tennis, for instance. If you play properly you will be so absorbed in the game that you will have no time to mope. Brains, like bodies, get tired. And for a tired brain there is nothing like fresh air, sunshine, cheerful companionship, and absorption in something that, for once, does not matter.

You will return from such a change with invigorated mental powers. You will see fresh points of view, and you will be pleasantly surprised to find that you have left the "blues" behind you.

Those Nerves

It has become rather fashionable these days to put everything down to "nerves." Frequently, people who are "nervy" are rather proud of the fact.

I suspect they have a vague idea that it denotes temperament, sensitiveness, refinement, ideas rather out of the common. The blunt truth is that such people are just an unholy nuisance to themselves and everyone else.

When people who are restless and irritable put it down to "nerves," they are talking nonsense. In a great many cases it is due to nothing more serious than indigestion. In any case, there's nothing to be proud about. If it isn't indigestion it is just simple lack of control.

A man may either be master of his mind or let his mind master him. You admit the necessity for controlling the mind in order to do efficient work? Then why not learn to control it in order to rest efficiently?

If trivial details that go wrong cause your temper to boil over, believe me, it is not "nerves"; it is lack of control, due to not knowing how and when to rest. And believe me, moreover, there is nothing to be proud of in being easily rattled.

When you rest, do it properly. Relax all your limbs: make your body comfortable. Make your mind equally comfortable. Remember that most of the things you are worrying about haven't happened yet!

No engine can work for ever at top speed. Set apart a little time each day for pure rest. The mental engine occasionally needs oiling; and the best oil is tranquillity.

People who have learned to control their minds don't suffer from "nerves."

Think Straight

There are a good many people who; while they would indignantly deny that they suffer from "nerves," are incorrigible worriers. They not only worry about their own affairs, but about the affairs of everyone connected with them.

They assume full responsibility for the plans of their families and friends; they take their mistakes on to their own shoulders; they spend a great deal of time, not in their own present, but in other people's futures.

It is not that they are simply incurable pessimists. True, they invariably see the worst in every situation, but on top of this they insist on adding to one's own worries—which are often real enough—their worries, which are too often purely artificial.

This time the trouble is not lack of mental control. It is simply crooked thinking. It is a form of mental laziness, an unwillingness to think out the true values of facts and their real relations. Such worrying helps nobody, not even the worrier.

Nearly always it ends in irritation and bad temper. Life is long, and the world is a big place. Trivial mistakes aren't worth the emotion your worrier expends on them. Past errors and future fears are alike worthless as subjects for thought.

The sort of person I am speaking of is at heart rather selfish, rather self-centred. Everything is considered in one light only: "How is it going to affect me?" No wonder they think crooked! Does the cap fit? Then get outside yourself. Make yourself a transmitter of ideas instead of a passive receiver of them.

Make an effort to see things in their true values. What's the use of pretending that every mouse is an elephant?

How to Make Money

Has it ever struck you what a lot of time most of us waste in useless envy of our neighbours? And in useless endeavours to be like them?

"Miss X has made a wonderful success as an actress. Why shouldn't I? Mr. Jones has made a fortune by writing. Why shouldn't I do the same?" We've all heard this sort of thing. Most of us have said it.

It is one of the greatest fallacies of human nature to try to do something merely because someone else has made a success of it. But for one who succeeds in this task of envious imitation there are a thousand who fail.

If you ask me why, I reply that you are You, and Miss X is Miss X. It is such a simple answer that we are apt to overlook it. Put yourself under the microscope. Somewhere in your composition there is some power, some combination of qualities, that marks you out from the rest of the world.

There is in everybody the possibility of originality, and the world is eagerly waiting for your contribution. Analyse yourself. Forget what other people are doing. Realise that Miss X and Mr. Jones are making fortunes because they have found the job they can do best—and are doing it.

Find the job you can do best. There are no rewards for the man who is content to remain in the rut. Somewhere in you is the thing for which the world is waiting. Find it. Dig it out. It will be worth money to you, for, because you are You—and no one else is exactly like you—it will be unique.

That is what the world pays heavily for.

The Holiday Mind

This month thousands of my readers will be having their holidays. I want them to have real holidays.

From the viewpoint of psychology a holiday is more than a mere search for pleasure and amusement: more than a relief from the routine of daily work: more than a renewal of bodily health. A real holiday is the achievement of a completely care-free mind.

Unless you can realise that, your holiday will not do you very much good. You go away to get a change of air, a change of scenery, a change of life. Don't take a scrap of your everyday life with you.

Forget there is such a thing as memory. Cultivate forgetfulness! Too many people take excess luggage with them in the shape of business and home worries. Believe me, they pay heavily for it.

Once you step into the train forget you ever had any work to do. Forget those unpaid bills; don't give a single thought to the worries and difficulties of the week after next. Give politics a rest. Forget there is such a thing as a newspaper. Most of us live too much in the future: a few live too much in the past.

Just for once live entirely in the present. Get back to the days when you were young, when you were content to let others do the worrying for you. Holiday time is the one time in the year when mental slackness is a virtue.

Delicate machinery is given a holiday periodically, for even steel gets tired. Give the infinitely delicate machinery of your mind a holiday.

Just for once don't think, just **BE**. That is the true holiday mind.

Character Building

The importance of character formation is responsible for an extraordinary amount of muddled thinking and useless advice.

It is, for instance, a nonsensical idea that men can be made decent, efficient, and good by sermons, lessons, and good resolutions. It is a very common error to assume that there is some mysterious influence in such things that operates mechanically in effecting a miraculous change.

If we were pure "thought machines," such things would be all right. Unfortunately, we all find it easier to act than to think. Character is simply the connections we make between our mental states and our acts. People who pin their faith to sermons, moral precepts, and the like forget that the only way to have these connections is to manufacture them deliberately.

A man's character cannot be made for him. His fate lies in his own hands. The only cure for laziness, for example, is the concrete act of work. Laziness and industry are both habits. It is entirely in our own hands whether we form the one or the other.

You cannot make a liar tell the truth by preaching at him. He must form the habit of telling the truth. We can only become efficient by behaving efficiently. All this is linked up with the question of self-control and will-power, which we shall have to consider later.

Meanwhile there are one or two broad principles we can lay down. Energy used in guiding and restraining conduct is more valuable than "hustle" for its own sake. There is no virtue in doing something merely because it is hard: effort for its own sake is wasted energy.

Lastly, "thought before action" is a golden rule.

Human Donkeys

Clearly, as I indicated last week, the will is of supreme importance where character is concerned. Before we consider how will-power can be developed, let us be quite clear as to what it is.

Far too many people think that obstinacy is a sign of a strong will. There are innumerable people who give lifelike imitations of human donkeys, and mistakenly pride themselves on it. Whether he goes on four legs or on two, a donkey is an ass. And an obstinate donkey is simply an obstinate ass.

The truth is that an obstinate man is nearly always, at bottom, a weak man: someone who cannot control either his thoughts or his emotions: a man who lacks a sense of proportion.

No; obstinacy is not will-power. Let us explore another fallacy while we are about it, that of the "strong, silent man."

I am always suspicious of these "strong, silent men." I fancy they are usually silent because they have nothing to say. A strong will, ably controlled and perfectly functioning, would not allow its owner to be perpetually silent. Decisive thought inevitably leads to decisive speech and action.

One of the surest signs of a weak will is the inability to come to a decision. From another angle it can be seen in the inability to carry out a decision that has been made.

Spend a few moments being honest with yourself. Are these signs observable in yourself? If they are, you need to take yourself in hand to train your will, to develop your will-power. Perhaps you are a human donkey? You also need to set about transforming a weak will into a strong one.

There is a way, as we shall see.

The Power-House

The importance of will-power cannot be exaggerated. The will is the power-house of the human machine. Will-power is the great motive force that lies behind every activity of the body or the mind.

It is given to few of us to be of the truly heroic cast of mind, the type of mind that combines iron willpower with sound reason. Nevertheless, it is an ideal to be aimed at, and the nearer we get to it the easier life becomes.

"Our strength and our intelligence, our wealth and even our good luck," says [8]Professor James, "are things that warm our hearts and make us feel ourselves a match for life. But deeper than all such things, and able to suffice unto itself without them, is the sense of the amount of effort which we can put forth."

In other words it is the consciousness of a strong, well-disciplined will that enables even the man who is "down and out" to rise again and battle with the world and win.

"He who can make no such effort," says the same writer, "is a shadow: he who can make much is a hero."

The game of life, particularly in these days, is no child's play. It is a game for men who can stand up to the world, who can keep their hearts unshaken and their heads erect. In the long run the amount of effort we can put forth, the measure of our will-power, is the measure of our worth as men.

The world is what we make it. Life is what we will have it. Unless we don the armour of a strong will we walk ever on the "perilous edge."

Will-power alone can carve a path to success. It is worth an effort to attain.

---

[8] Professor William James-Psychologist (1842-1910)

Eyes Front!

One of the commonest characteristics of the weak man is the fatal tendency to have "back thoughts."

Set-backs come to everyone. We all make mistakes. Business failures, plans going awry, these are the common lot. Your weak man sinks under them: your strong man smiles—a trifle bitterly, maybe —and plods on.

What is the difference? Simply that the weak man keeps his eyes turned towards the past, fills his mind with vain regrets. The strong man keeps his eyes to the future, his thoughts on the goal to be attained.

The one broods over the failures as failures; the other counts them as valuable lessons learned, as additions to the dearly-bought experience that will bring him in the end to his desire. Thought uncontrolled is a deadly enemy to willpower. Think by all means, but think forward; think constructively.

Build for the future. There is nothing gained by mournful contemplation of the ruins of the past. "The best is yet to be," sang [9]Robert Browning, "the last of life for which the first was made." It is a sound motto for anyone who feels weak-willed and wishes to take himself in hand.

In fact, the first lesson in the education of the will is to learn to balance our mental powers—and take care to let the balance sway towards an optimistic outlook on life. Half the battle in controlling the will is not in doing positive acts, but in refusing to do them.

The difficulty is not to be optimistic, but to prevent oneself being pessimistic. Anyone can yield to a temptation: the battle comes in refusing to yield.

"The best is yet to be." Remember that, and be of good heart.

---

[9] Robert Browning (1812-1889) English poet. Taken from his epic poem Rabbi Ben Ezra.

Exercising the Will

I have frequently referred in these articles to the question of habit formation. Nowhere is it more important than in the ease of training the will.

Habit can be stated to be the tendency to repeat automatically acts—whether mental or physical—that we have performed in the past. If we continually find ourselves doing something we know perfectly well we ought not to do, or not doing something we know we should do, the cause is simple.

Call it a weak will if you like: more simply it is just lack of practice. How does a poor batsman make himself into a county player? Just practice. He plods away until he has formed the habit of playing with a straight bat, formed the habit of playing his strokes correctly, and making eye and wrist work in perfect unison.

Nothing else but a long series of repeated acts has been responsible—plus a good deal of determination to succeed. Tackle the problem of will-power on similar lines. If you desire strong muscles you exercise them. If you desire a strong will you exercise that too.

It is not enough to have a half-hearted idea that you will strengthen your will. Think the matter out in detail. Weigh up your difficulties. Start the process by a clear vision of what you have to do, and a strong determination to see the thing through.

More, be as serious about it on Tuesday as you were on Monday. The discipline of practice demands unremitting endeavour if it is to be successful.

Don't forget to suggest to yourself continually that you are improving. Such suggestions are a powerful ally.

The Concrete Problem

Let us get right down to this question of training the will. What, in other words, is your particular problem?

For the will is not a concrete object that can be exercised and trained in itself as a particular muscle can be exercised and trained. It is far more a nice balance of mental powers, a proper use of mental powers, an adjustment of mental forces.

Think it over: have a quiet half-hour with yourself, and do not shirk exposing your weaknesses. Somewhere a concrete problem faces you—maybe several. You may wish to overcome a habit—smoking for example. You may wish to pursue certain studies, and find yourself weakly postponing the time when you will begin.

These are the sort of things I mean when I talk about training the will; for it is just such problems as these that disclose your strength or your weakness. Don't, therefore, waste your time by trying to develop will-power in general.

Concentrate on your weak point. If it is cigarette smoking, set about the difficult task of substituting a good habit for a bad one.

In fact, try to cultivate the habit of self-control. Keep steadily in front of you the concrete aim you have in view. Don't say, "I must strengthen my will." Say instead, "I must give up cigarette smoking."

To be successful you must cultivate a positive outlook. Your task is to become a non-smoker, not to stop smoking. This may sound a subtle distinction, but there is a world of difference between the two points of view.

The strong-willed man is, at bottom, the man who can face battles like this and win them. And each time such a fight is won the will is strengthened enormously.

The Cross-Roads

If you will look back at what I had to say some weeks ago about Memory, you will find that I was continually urging you to think.

To think, to concentrate, to make an effort of attention, to hold fast to an idea or pursue a train of thought without allowing the mind to be diverted—here you have the secret of memory.

Here also you have the secret of the will. How often does the man of weak will, of indecisive mind, say when confronted with the results of his weakness, "I didn't think?"

'What a miserable excuse it is! If you "didn't think," the only adequate retort is, "Why didn't you think? Why? Why? Why?"

What else raises you above the animal except the power to think? What else distinguishes you from the rest of creation except the possession of a brain that can think and reason and decide?

If you don't think, you are intellectually lazy, and I have yet to hear any valid excuse for mental sloth. It is your duty to think: and it is your duty to think rightly.

That we "needs must know the Highest when we see it "may not be strictly true, but unless we are completely lost in mental and moral apathy, the Highest cannot fail to stir a responsive note in us.

An "Act of will" involves a choice: it means, very often, the suppression of desire; it demands a careful sifting of values; it calls for a forgetfulness of self and a consideration of larger issues. No one can live unto himself alone. Every act affects someone else. To see consequences clearly is an enormous help to right decision.

If you can vision the end, the way will be made plain.

Men as Gods

It is characteristic of the human machine that it is full of contradictions. Take sight, for example.

The human eye—regarded simply as a piece of mechanism—would be unhesitatingly condemned by any self-respecting optician. Mechanically, it is open to criticism at almost every point. Yet, when it comes to seeing, its ability to perform its work is miraculous.

So with the more intangible yet equally potent attributes of the machine. Side by side with incredible strength we find incredible weakness.

It is a curious paradox that a mind and a brain capable of overcoming terrific obstacles, of guiding the destinies of nations or subjugating Nature to its will, not infrequently finds itself incapable of resisting quite minor temptations.

Weakness is not a thing of which we need be ashamed. But there is no greater shame than to allow this weakness to conquer us.

Inherent in our make-up are infinite possibilities. We are weak or we are strong just in so far as we dominate our circumstances or allow circumstances to be our master. Not that to ride rough-shod over everybody and everything is necessarily a mark of the strong man.

Often it is merely the mark of the bully, the dully obstinate and unreasoning, the selfish and unfeeling. The Caesars, Napoleons, and Mussolinis of the world count for little beside the Platos, the Socrates, and the Christs.

Small wonder it has been said that man is but a little lower than the angels, since he can reason and choose. Man is master of his fate. He can shape the world to his own ends. But he can only do this by the conscious realisation that his will is both his sword and his shield.

False Pride

If a delicate machine goes wrong, common sense suggests an inspection of the mechanism to find out where the fault lies.

Common sense likewise suggests that the mechanism should be inspected by a man who knows all about it. It is surprising how few people think of applying such common-sense methods to the delicate machinery of their own minds.

Ill-temper, sulkiness, indecision, morbidity, all these things and many more are signs of a temporary breakdown of the mental machinery. In nine cases out of ten the trouble is an idea or a set of thoughts acting like grit in the wheels.

It's often very useful to have a look inside the mind. It frequently makes all the difference between gloom and happiness. A little occasional self-analysis—but not too much— is an excellent thing.

False pride is frequently the dirt in the machinery— the false pride that will not allow you to own yourself in the wrong although you know well that the fault is yours. The result is that you brood. Fancied grievances begin to take on an air of reality. You soon begin to look at the world through black spectacles. And you make yourself and everyone else thoroughly miserable.

It is one of the infallible signs of the strong man that he is never afraid to confess he has made a mistake. He has too much self-respect to indulge in self-deception, too much respect for others to allow misunderstandings to continue when a word can put matters right.

Next time things go wrong and the world begins to look black, see if the fault isn't yours. And be strong enough to "own up."

The Lighted Way

From time to time I have pointed out various mental powers that, rightly used, act as a spur and a source of energy. Did it ever occur to you what a help imagination can be, if directed towards the right ends? We all know people of whom it can truly be said, "They are quite devoid of imagination."

As a rule this is nothing to their discredit. Quite often there goes along with this lack an equable temper, a placid temperament, a calm that neither joy nor adversity can readily destroy. But you will rarely find that a person who lacks imagination gets anywhere. He moves always in a limited space. He gets in a rut—and is content to stay there.

[10]"Where there is no vision," said the old writer, "the people perish." And without imagination there comes also a mental and spiritual death. Dulled imagination means dulled desire, dulled ambition, the death of endeavour and enterprise. But imagination should be directed towards a positive and constructive end. Picture what might be, picture what you want to be.

Use your imagination as a torch to light a difficult and unknown path. Some people use their imagination to picture all the obstacles and terrors they may—perhaps—encounter. To do that is to misuse a valuable faculty. It is to transform into a brake what could, and should, be a motive force. Neither should imagination be allowed to develop into mere day-dreaming. To do that is merely to allow it to drain away mental energy that could be far better employed.

No great man ever became great without using imagination. Remember that — and keep out of the rut.

---

[10] Bible – Proverbs 29:18

Day Dreams

Last week I had something to say about the value of cultivating a vivid imagination. Let us carry that topic a little further.

What is known as "day-dreaming" is another aspect of it. Everyone day-dreams at times; some do it to such an extent that they become unpractical, moody, out of touch with realities; others only do it on rare occasions.

But I doubt if there is anyone who at some time or another has not indulged in this pleasantly soothing occupation. Like so many other forms of mental activity its value depends entirely on the use made of it—-on the way the energy is directed.

Certainly day-dreaming can be either an inspiration or a vice. It all depends, as is so often the case, whether you make it your servant or allow it to become your master. To sit and simply pursue aimless and idle trains of thought, unless they be definitely and deliberately undertaken as a form of mental rest and recreation, is to use day-dreaming as a drug.

Even so, it has its place, if used sparingly and with discretion: but do not allow it to become a habit. The sort of day-dreaming that is really valuable is when one sits down and deliberately visions what might be, when one reviews the past, considers the present, and builds the future.

It was such dreams and visions that led Columbus to America that gave Newton the secret of gravitation that inspired every great man who has ever left his mark on history. Don't be afraid of such dreams. They can be made the spur to action and the accomplishment of big things.

But never allow them to be more than a prelude. The thing that matters is the action they inspire.

On Guard!

We have just passed through a flood of oratory and argument that is an object-lesson to anyone interested in the workings of the human mind.

On all sides we have seen men of unquestionable honesty deceiving themselves and others with the best intentions in the world. The truth is that beliefs, and the arguments we bring forward to support them, are in most cases irrational.

Rational and logical thought, the sifting of facts and the weighing of evidence with an unbiassed mind, are some of the most difficult things for the ordinary person to accomplish. Self-deception is terribly easy.

"Give your decision," said the old hand to the newly created judge; "it will probably be right. But do not give your reasons, for they will almost certainly be wrong."

Any of us, when taxed with an obvious discrepancy between our principles and our conduct, will at once produce a beautiful set of reasons to justify what we have done. But nearly always the reasons are an afterthought, a mere piece of self-deception and self- justification.

We would do well to make a steady practice of attempting to view facts dispassionately. Mental honesty and a disciplined mind are two aspects of the same thing. How often do we hear it said of a person that his judgment is" sound"? Such a man is always admired and trusted by his colleagues.

We are all too prone to take our opinions ready-made. We should all be more willing to think for ourselves. The facts of life are there for everyone to observe. Keep an open mind. Observe, weigh, and consider.

And base your opinions on facts. If you refuse to deceive yourself, others will find it hard to deceive you.

Danger!

From one point of view these articles may all be regarded as so many signposts along the road to efficiency and success. Let me, this week, erect a different sort of signpost. Let me put up a danger signal. It is one of the queer traits of the human being that the attainment of success all too frequently leads to disappointment and disaster.

Look, for instance, at politicians. How often do 'we see a man who, brilliant, forceful, and dominating in opposition, becomes an ineffective cypher when he assumes command of the Government? We read the lesson in his case, because the [11]"fierce light that beats about a throne" throws every detail into relief. Too often we fail to see the parallel in our own lives. Success is a heady wine that not infrequently acts as an anaesthetic to initiative. The fight's the thing! Instinctively man is a pugnacious animal, always spoiling for a fight, whether it be in his own cause or that of someone else. Pugnacity is an instinct: every endeavour that is based on instinct is double-armed. It has an inexhaustible supply of energy behind it. But, mentally or physically, we can't stand still. If we don't go forward, we slide backwards. In common with the whole of Nature we must keep on moving. That is the danger of success. We imagine it means rest, final attainment, a definite end. Nothing of the kind! Successful achievement should involve a change of direction for our energies. Unless the fight is maintained there can only result a period of stagnation, followed by decay.

Don't be drugged into apathy by success. It is the tragedy of nearly every great man.

---

[11] From Idylls of the King by English poet Alfred Lord Tennyson (1809-1892).

Look Outwards

The Americans have a phrase whereby they describe a man as "a good mixer"; a man, that is, who is at home in any society, who "gets on" with anyone with whom he is thrown into contact.

There is no secret about such a man. It is, I grant you, partly a matter of personal characteristics, but it is still more a question of adaptability. If we dug a little deeper still we should find it was also a question of being able to see the other person's point of view.

There is one characteristic that is outstanding about the human machine—its well-nigh limitless power of adaptation to circumstances and to emergencies. It is a power that it pays everyone to be fully conscious of. That it behoves us all to train and use.

If we turn all our thoughts inward to ourselves we shall find it very difficult to adapt ourselves. It can only be done by continually thinking outwards, as it were.

Your self-centred man, whose first and only question when confronted by a new situation is, "How is this going to affect me?" can never be a good mixer. He erects a wall of selfishness between himself and others. He implies that there can be no other viewpoint than his own.

He broods over fancied wrongs, becomes suspicious, indulges in self-pity. The remedy is to be interested in people, to lend a receptive mind to their views and opinions, and to realise that people are interested in you in the same way.

Remember, too, that what seems so important to you may be negligible to someone else. Cultivate a sense of perspective. Try putting yourself in the other fellow's place. You're not the only person in the world!

Amoeba— Men

The lowest and simplest form of life on this planet consists of a single cell. It is a complete unity, all-sufficient to itself, caring nothing for, and desiring nothing of, its neighbours.

The Amoeba, as this cell is named, is certainly alive in the physical sense. In its own way it is a perfectly functioning machine. But "existence" is a fitter name for its state than "life."

The human machine, likewise perfectly functioning, needs more than a state of mere existence if it is to develop. If a man is ever to be more than a possibility, he needs life in its fullest sense. He needs, in fact, the reflex of other lives, the constant reaction of other personalities.

If, like the Amoeba, he lives in a world bounded by his own consciousness, giving nothing, receiving nothing from his fellows, he stunts his mental and spiritual force.

He will still, of course, have an individuality, a personal consciousness that is his alone: but it cannot develop. All such self-centred and self-sufficient people are strangely alike. They are as uniform—and as uninteresting—as a row of worms would be.

It is contact with others, interchange of views and ideas, "rubbing shoulders," as they say, that ultimately brings out and ripens a man's speciality and real individuality that distinguishes him from every other human being.

And it is this association alone that can develop the force that binds millions into a church, a movement, an embodied idea that can alter history and change the face of the world. "One Englishman is a fool," said a recent writer, "two are a match, three are a great nation."

There is a tremendous lesson in this epigram for any man who is complacently content to imitate the Amoeba.

The Physical Base

It is as well to remember that all the effort and training in the world will not produce an efficient mind unless the bodily side receives attention.

After all, the body—with its nerves and muscles, its arteries, and its delicate co-ordinations—is the instrument through which the mind must function. If the instrument is faulty, the results—so far as the mind is concerned—must inevitably be poor.

What often appears as weak will, for instance, may really be due to poor physical health. Inability to concentrate may often be due to defective eye—sight. It is of the highest importance, therefore, to train the body as carefully and as scientifically as we train the mind.

Adequate food, sound sleep—and plenty of it— and a sufficiency of exercise are absolutely essential to attain the ideal of "a healthy mind in a healthy body." A prompt rise from bed upon awaking, followed by a few minutes of smart physical exercises, give a tone and a vim to the body that cannot fail to have a favourable effect on the mind.

These simple morning exercises will, if tackled systematically, train the mind as well. They will, for instance, directly develop willpower. There will be many mornings when it would be much pleasanter to stay a few moments more in bed. Each time you resist the temptation you have done a good deal towards strengthening your will.

Above all, you will be laying the essential physical foundation for any mental training you attempt.

Fear

Roughly speaking, it can be said that our mental life, and particularly our powers of creative thought, enable us to adapt our conduct to our environment.

The man who uses his brain aright, and who has learned how to direct his thoughts, behaves intelligently when faced with difficult or unexpected situations, instead of blundering around in a blind endeavour to find a way out.

But thought, like every other function of the human machine, can at times lead us sadly astray unless we keep it under control. Just as the blood can both keep us healthy and at the same time serve as a medium for disease, so our thought can be both useful and a medium for serious blunders.

It all depends on the measure of control we achieve over its direction. When thought turns in the direction of unreasoning fear it is performing a useless function. It becomes a serious hindrance to activity, a source of worry and anxiety, a steady drain on energy and initiative.

Fear, based on something that is, more often than not, entirely imaginary is a common enough experience. And the trouble is that what appears trivial to the outsider seems very real indeed to the person concerned.

There is only one thing to be done if you are obsessed by a continual dread. Face it boldly, analyse it, lay bare its roots and discover if there is any real foundation for it. Few fears can live beneath the searchlights of cold fact.

But you will have to be honest with yourself, own up to your own insincerities, and have the courage to laugh at yourself for your timidity. Certainly the sure way to clothe the skeleton of fear with flesh is to be afraid of it!

Courage

Writing on "Character Building" some weeks ago I said, "We can only become efficient by behaving efficiently." Let us look further at the question of Fear, and apply this maxim to it.

There would be no problem if fears could always be banished by saying boldly, "I am not afraid. I have no fears." A good many of them can, if this suggestion is continually used, believed, and relied on, but not all.

The surest way to conquer fear is to cultivate courage. It is the difference we have met with before between a positive and a negative outlook on life. It is the pessimist who fears, and lags behind. The optimist hopes, and goes forward unafraid.

Many people are painfully self-depreciatory of their abilities and powers, and of their value to the world. They give themselves credit for very little.

It is this self-depreciation that so often induces undue sensitiveness, timidity, and fear. A certain school that proudly flaunts the motto, "Believing in myself, what is there I cannot accomplish?" has come very near the root of the fear problem. And it has certainly disclosed the secret of courage.

True courage, the ability to forge ahead in the face of known or imagined obstacles, demands will-power, purpose and sincerity. No one can be courageous who is insincere; and to be honest with oneself is as important as to be honest with others.

Believe in yourself, believe in the purpose that inspires your thought and your action, believe in the promise of the future, and place less reliance on its threats—attune your mind to a constructive and positive view of your place in life, and you will develop courage all right.

And as courage develops, so will fear vanish.

Facing Fear

Writing to me about my remarks on fear, a correspondent says: "For weeks I have put off having a tooth extracted because of the fear it causes me. I know I am foolish. I realise that I am not frightened of having gas. I don't really mind the thought of having the tooth out. Yet looked at as a whole, the operation frightens me so much that week after week passes without my going to the dentist. What am I to do?"

The lady who writes thus has really answered her own question. She has tackled her fear in the right way, but has failed to realise it, and so has not made any use of her knowledge. Writing on "Fear" I said: "Face it boldly, analyse it, lay bare its roots, and discover if there is any real foundation for it."

My correspondent has done this. Does she fear taking gas? Clearly not. Does she fear the actual extraction? She admits that she does not. What does she fear? She has discovered that the fear—if she tackles each part separately—loses its power. Her mistake is to slip back from this little analysis to a vague, general idea that is terrifying just because it is vague.

The fear comes from the vagueness, the inherent terror of the unknown, plus, I have no doubt, a number of unpleasant recollections.

Her remedy is (1) to try to forget any past experiences; (2) to stand by her analysis and face each part of the problem separately; (3) to realise that every element of the problem is known to her. There is no vague "something" concerned that she cannot define; (4) to keep her thoughts strictly within these limits.

Such an attack on a fear reduces it to its proper proportions.

Courage and Fear

Here is a problem that is certainly not confined to my correspondent. Her fear is no doubt common to hundreds of my readers at the present time.

"My husband works very late," she writes, "and there have been so many burglaries in this district that I am terrified at being left alone. All I can do is to sit and wait for the door to be opened. "I tried wedging the door with a chair, but it was no better. Instead of watching the door, I now watch the chair, and sit waiting for it to move."

It is no use, of course, to do as my correspondent has done, and merely replace one fear by another. By using the chair she has (1) admitted the reality of her fear; (2) focussed it even more definitely than before.

Now I happen to know the district where this lady lives. She lives in a flat. There are neighbours above and below. Let her fix her mind on the fact that she is surrounded by friends within easy call. Next, the burglaries in her district have not occurred anywhere near her flat. Her road is particularly well patrolled by the police—another positive fact on which to fix her mind.

Let her face her fear on these lines, putting against a vague uneasiness all the positive facts on the other side that will bring comfort to her mind. There will be far more such facts. In itself, each may be of only small value. Taken together, I fancy they will amount to a good deal.

It is always the vague sense of fear that is the hardest to bear. Put it in the balance against hard facts. You will be surprised at its insignificance.

The Open Door

A proverb which is not, perhaps, universally true states that "there is no time like the present."

When it comes to tackling a haunting fear it is the truest thing that could be said. Remember that all fears are of the future. It is the uncertainty that kills. We spend half our time being miserable about something that has not yet happened— and may never happen.

And this, incidentally, is a fact that should be realised whenever fear obtrudes its ugly head. But if you find a fear haunting you, don't delay facing up to it for a minute. The longer you delay the worse it will be, and the harder your task of analysis will grow.

Delay allows imagination to take a hand, and imagination has a habit of looking at fear through a magnifying-glass. Moreover, if you delay your estimation of true and false values, you allow your whole stream of thought to be poisoned at the source.

No good gardener allows an ugly weed to flourish unchecked. He roots it up before it has time to seed and double his labour. Fear is an exceptionally ugly weed— and its roots go deep. Don't give it a chance to develop.

If you think about one thing too much you end by thinking in circles. Your thought loses force, loses direction. The quickest way out of such a circle is to step out—-boldly. The person obsessed by fear is like the forgotten prisoner who remained in his cell for ten years, until it occurred to him one day to open the door and escape.

There is no time like the present.

Holding Your Own

Several readers have written to me asking me to devote some space to the question, "How can I rid myself of nervousness?" They mean, of course, "How can I develop confidence in myself? How can I substitute self-confidence for a shrinking self-depreciation?

I will, this week, content myself with some general preliminary observations. Not infrequently this nervousness, paradoxical though it may seem, springs in reality from an exaggerated sense of self-importance. We imagine that everyone's eyes are on us, that we are the centre of attention, and that our appearance, acts, and words are of supreme interest to friends, acquaintances, and strangers.

The truth is quite otherwise. Most people are far too occupied with their own thoughts and their own affairs to bother much about other people. Therefore, get rid of the idea that you are the only person of whom other folk are thinking. They are not thinking about you nearly as much as you are thinking about yourself.

It is really a point I have occasionally touched on before. Nervousness tends to come when one's thoughts are continually turned inwards instead of outwards. It is the result of self-analysis that has been continued until it has become morbid.

A famous writer once said to an aspiring young journalist: "Remember that there is at least a guinea article in every person you meet." He meant that everybody has some point of interest or some special piece of knowledge that is peculiarly his own. That applies to you too.

If you find other people interesting, you may depend upon it they find you interesting. Your ideas, your point of view, may seem worth little to you. To other people they are probably original and stimulating.

To realise this is the first step.

Self- Realisation

Lack of self-confidence very often means lack of self-knowledge. The man who is ill at ease in the company of others is, more often than not, a man who has failed to realise his own potentialities.

There is a law of human behaviour that we all fail to observe from time to time. It is that we must give out in proportion as we take in. We must see that the knowledge, the experience, the energy that we absorb is allowed to flow out again in some way.

Otherwise, we turn our minds into choked drains, whereas they should be clear channels for the easy flow of thoughts and ideas.

[12]Macaulay once characterised schoolboys as "books in breeches." Too often when we grow up we are still "books in breeches," still—as [13]Pope expressed it:
> "A lumber-house of books in every head,
> Forever reading, never to be read! "

Physical indigestion is apt to give us a very sour view of the world. Mental indigestion is apt to do the same thing. It is as well for the man who lacks confidence to make sure that he is not accusing his fellows of the scorn and contempt that resides, in reality, in his own mind!

Somehow or other the shy and diffident individual must endeavour to find a medium of self-expression. He must try to discover ways of self-realisation. He must cultivate an active, instead of a passive, attitude of mind.

Take letter-writing, for instance. If you find it difficult to talk to a person, write to him. Next time you meet you will have a common interest ready-made.

Self-expression is the key to self-confidence,

---

[12] From Lady Holland's Memoir, Volume 1, by Sydney Smith (1769-1845).
[13] From The Dunciad by Alexander Pope (1688-1744).

Self-Development

In order to overcome a lack of self-confidence it is essential to realise—and to believe—that it is a mental attitude that can be cured.

Trite as this sounds, it is necessary to stress it. So many of my correspondents seem to think that in their case there is nothing to be done, although others may be successful. Note carefully those words "a mental attitude," for while I admit that poor physical health may be a contributory cause, shyness and timidity are things of the mind and call for mental measures.

That is why I speak of "self-development." It is your mental attitude that needs correction if you lack confidence, and "self-help" is the only kind that is of any avail. Attend to the physical side by all means. An unhealthy body cannot fail to react unfavourably on the mind.

Like all problems, analysis is the first need. Self-knowledge must precede self-development. Don't blunder vaguely in the dark. No one lacks confidence at all points. Find out very exactly just where the trouble lies.

Then tackle the difficulties one at a time. Do you mistrust your abilities? There is some hobby, possibly, at which you shine—proof that along certain lines your capability is sound. If you can do that, you can do other things equally well—given interest and practice.

There must be some people with whom you are not shy. Isn't it, again, interest? This time, a community of interest? Next time you meet anyone, try to discover some common ground. You will forget to be shy.

Self-development means a search for interest. Lack of confidence implies weak mental" muscles." Exercise them and make them strong.

Never Say Die!

A good many people who think they lack self-confidence would find, with a little closer thought, that their real trouble is an overplus of self-consciousness. In many cases such self-consciousness has its root in the existence of some physical defect—such as lameness, stammering, and the like. The victim is so conscious of his disability that he feels sure everyone else is equally conscious of it. It acts as a drag on all his activities, as a constant drain on his energies. In the end he probably pities himself hugely. And by doing this he helps no one—not even himself. Self-pity merely manufactures hatred—hatred of one's fellows, of the world, of life.

Yet the sufferer might well take heart of grace as he looks through history. [14]Demosthenes will be famous for all time as the silver-tongued orator of ancient Greece. Yet Demosthenes stammered! [15]Mozart, one of Music's Immortals, did not let his disability stifle his genius. For Mozart had a defective ear! [16]Byron had a club foot; [17]Pope was a cripple; [18]Milton did his greatest work after he lost his sight. One and all they refused to be hampered. They wasted no time in self-pity. They refused to be self-conscious. But there are too many people to whom [19]Emerson's words would apply: "What you are stands over you and thunders so that I cannot hear what you say to the contrary." **Don't let what you are blacken life with its shadow. Let what you will be, what you can be, guide your endeavours and your thoughts. If you lack in one direction, be sure you can weigh down the balance in another. Obstacles can be overcome.**

After all, what the world wants are the gifts you have-it cares nothing for those you lack.

---

[14] Demosthenes – Greek Statesman (384-322 BC).
[15] Wolfgang Amadeus Mozart – (1756-1791).
[16] George Gordon Byron – English Poet, (1788-1824).
[17] Alexander Pope – (1688-1744) Crippled at age 12 through an infection that affected his spine.
[18] John Milton – English poet, (1608-1674). Milton was completely blind by the age of 43.
[19] Ralph Waldo Emerson – (1803-1882). American lecturer famous for his essays and pioneering thought on individuality and freedom.

The Uphill Road

To those of my readers who attempt to put into practice the various hints and aids to efficiency that appear from time to time in these articles, I want to offer a word of warning and advice.

Don't expect to succeed all at once. Don't be either disappointed or surprised if, after a few hours or a few days, you have not succeeded in effecting any marked improvement. In nearly every instance it is a case of eradicating a bad habit and putting a good habit in its place.

You cannot, for instance, expect to replace an indecisive mind by strength of will and decision in twenty-four hours.

For years you have formed the habit of hesitation, doubt, and worry, until it has become firmly rooted. Make no mistake. It is going to be a tough fight to uproot it. Self-conquest is never easy.

And the first thing to do is to realise the strength of the forces arrayed against you, so that your efforts to overcome them may, in their turn, be sufficiently strong.

And then, if after the lapse of months, if after months of steady practice you begin to notice a little improvement, believe me you will have every reason to congratulate yourself on having fought a good fight.

Self-mastery involves an uphill fight every step of the way, a long fight in which victory can only be attained by patience, practice, and perseverance. There is only one sure method—the strongest possible attack, complete belief in your cause, and complete faith that in the end you will win.

And I fancy the last is the most important. For faith can still work miracles, if used intelligently.

Seek Your Self!

The problem of self-confidence hinges to a great extent on what one conceives to be one's true self. A man's self has many sides, and not all of them are of importance.

Any given side of a man's character may, in the course of a lifetime, be developed and become the distinguishing mark of that man. But it becomes real only in so far as the other sides, the other possibilities, are more or less suppressed.

The feeling of humiliation which those who lack confidence feel so keenly springs from failure. Something has been attempted, the result is poor and unsatisfactory, and the inevitable comparison arises with someone else who has done the same thing well.

It follows that it is of the highest importance to be sure that the self on which we stake all our hopes and aspirations is really the truest and deepest side of us. A calm and honest review of our powers and our desires is the true beginning of an attempt to increase confidence.

Ambition is indeed a wonderful lever; but be sure the urge is in a direction that accords with what you feel is in your power. And be sure, too, that the goal is worth the trouble of attaining. "Make thy claim of wages a zero," said Carlyle[20], "then hast thou the world under thy feet." Expect nothing, in other words, and you will not be disappointed! But any success you do achieve will be so much incentive to go forward to new conquests.

Distinguish, too, between those whose opinions of you matter and those whose criticism is idle interference. Not everybody has the power to hurt you—unless you over-rate your worth.

There is a lot in Carlyle's blunt remark: "I tell thee, blockhead, it all comes of thy vanity!"

---

[20] Thomas Carlyle – (1795-1881) Scottish philosopher and writer.

Well-fitting Tights

In one of the stories in [21]*Stalky & Co* Kipling describes what happened when a master suddenly descended upon a rowdy rehearsal for a schoolboy pantomime.

All the culprits felt—and looked—extremely foolish. All, that is, except Stalky himself, who faced the angry master coolly, "secure in the confidence born of his well-fitting tights." It is a little sidelight on the problem of self-confidence that will bear thinking about. It is not so trivial as it sounds.

Men find a great deal of amusement in the care a woman takes of her personal appearance, the close attention to detail, and the anxiety she displays to be at least as well dressed as any other woman she may meet. Nevertheless, the woman is the sounder psychologist of the two.

The mind is very readily coloured by its surroundings. It responds to "atmosphere," and the knowledge of a neat personal appearance has a subtle effect in engendering that confidence that enables a man to look his fellows in the face.

Neatness and pride of person is not the prerogative of women. A man can be well dressed, in the sense of being tidy, without being in any way an effeminate fool. He owes it to his self-respect to make the best of himself. Clothes certainly do not make the man, but they can be used as an avenue for the expression of personality.

An untidy mind is rarely so much a cause as an effect. And why ignore an aid to mental tidiness and efficiency that is directly within your power?

The "confidence born of well-fitting tights" is a psychological truth well known to every woman who buys a new hat. It is no less true in its application to men.

---

[21] Stalky & Co published in 1899, written by Rudyard Kipling (1865-1936).

Fighting To Win

Religion and science are still inclined to debate the question whether man is a fallen angel or a risen reptile. Be that as it may, psychology sees overwhelming evidence that the urge of a man's mental life is onwards and upwards.

There is an eternal struggle proceeding between the incalculable force of creative energy residing in every man and the tremendous repressive forces of society, conventions, moral barriers, and the like.

We are forever in a state of conflict, conflict which, as a psychologist says, "is the very root and source of life. Without conflict we could never have risen further in our nervous organisation than a series of reflex arcs, even if we could have lived at all."

Every time we meet a difficulty that calls for a battle between our higher and our lower selves, it is well to face it in the knowledge of what hangs on the outcome. If the battle is won, spiritual and mental energy is released from bondage to unworthy things, refined and spiritualised, and set free to achieve new adjustments on a higher plane of activity.

If the battle is lost, the whole personality sinks back into a lower plane, and the price is, not infrequently, an inner sense of shame, of loss of self-respect, a sense of failure that decreases the power of resistance when the next test comes.

Every conflict, mental or spiritual, should be fought to a finish. Nothing should be spared to achieve victory. That every advantage we gain merely becomes a battle-ground for new problems matters little. For be sure: the conflict will never cease. The thing to remember is that conflict is a sign of energy making desperate efforts to gain expression on a higher level. Knowing that, "Fight to win" should be a daily guide.

Leaders to Nowhere

The aim of these articles is to point out how the human machine can be made to function more effectively; to try to show how a man may climb out of the rut and do something worthwhile in the world.

When, however, a machine is keyed up to produce more and more power, it is necessary to have a clear idea to what the extra power is to be applied. Power without purpose is simply a senseless waste of energy.

There are too many men who want to lead, prizing leadership for its own sake, confusing the means with the end, worshipping Power without having the imagination to vision an ultimate end for that power.

They are leaders to nowhere, unless it be to disaster. "Once or twice in every generation," said a recent writer, "there lives a man who attempts a small task in a corner: and perceiving it clearly in its relative importance to the rest of existence, puts his nose to the grindstone—with his eyes open to the horizon— and does the thing."

We all have our noses to the grindstone: we have not always our eyes "open to the horizon" at the same time. That is why so much of our effort ends in futility.

No man should ever divorce imagination from his work. He should endeavour to see life clearly, and see it whole, and should fit his efforts into a scheme that has a very definite end in view. That is the real meaning of ambition.

And if your small task—even though it be done in a corner—leads somewhere, keep your nose to the grindstone. The danger lies in seeing no further than the grindstone. There is a wider horizon than that.

Automatic Machinery

From time to time I have mentioned in these articles the use that can be made of the subconscious mind.

As a method of reinforcing the formation of habits, of ridding the mind of unreal fears, strengthening the will, and countless other qualities, it has no equal if used intelligently. "Auto-suggestion," as the psychologists call it, suggestions made by oneself to oneself, is one of the most powerful forces in the world.

Always providing, of course, that the suggestion is made firmly and backed up by the conviction that it is going to be effective. The subconscious mind seizes on these suggestions, receives them with avidity, and—given the conditions stated in the previous paragraph—endeavours to carry them out continuously.

Moreover, the subconscious mind, unlike the conscious mind, never sleeps. All through the night the suggestion is working, taking hold, consolidating its position. This is why so many people advise "sleeping over it," when one is confronted by a difficult problem.

Their advice would be endorsed by any psychologist. The subconscious mind is a piece of automatic machinery, tireless, always at the service of anyone who cares to use it. Test it for yourself. All you have to do is to think out carefully the pros and cons of your problem before going to sleep—and then think no more about it.

You will nearly always find on awakening that the solution springs ready-made to your mind, for your subconscious mind will have been busy on it all the time your conscious mind was asleep.

The point to remember is that you cannot keep your subconscious mind idle. You might just as well, therefore, make deliberate use of it.

Playtime

I have before me as I write a number of letters from correspondents which deserve more than a passing reference.

"I am working so hard," says one, "that I have no time to read. In fact, it is six months since I opened a book for pleasure." Another says he has no time to spare for games. He is anxious to pass an examination—a laudable ambition —and every spare moment is devoted to study.

So they all say. The burden of these letters is "I have no time to play". How easy it is to confuse folly with wisdom! My correspondents are taking considerable pride in the fact that they are ill-treating their physical and mental machinery!

Play—in which I include every form of relaxation, be it reading, football, cycling, motoring, or even light conversation—is a sheer necessity to the human being. In fact, it is an instinct, and an instinct that cannot be thwarted without serious results.

There is a lot in the remark of Mr. Gordon Selfridge that "there is no fun like work"; but it is equally true that there is no medicine like play. The human machine must have rest from the constant drive of worry and anxiety. The most brilliant student I ever knew spent the three days before his final examination in playing cricket—and he romped home.

It was a fresh, braced-up brain that entered the examination room, instead of one jaded and stale for want of rest. Get out into the sunshine. Breathe the fresh air. Every now and again take an hour and "waste" it in play.

For if you work hard and play hard your work will, as Mr. Selfridge says, be fun. But you must play well in order to work well.

Think First

It is a commonplace that the power of thought distinguishes man from the other animals. What exactly is the object of this function of conscious thought?

Its object, it seems to me, is to enable man to gain a true knowledge of reality, to enable him to do the one thing that has made him master of the world— adapt himself to his environment.

In fact, as I have elsewhere stated, the surest test of a man's intelligence is the speed with which he can dominate and mould to his own will an unaccustomed set of circumstances. To put it even more simply, I believe a man's intelligence to be measured by the ease with which he overcomes difficulties.

Now there is a right way and a wrong way of using this tremendous weapon of conscious thought: we can either use it blindly, prodigally, wastefully, or direct it as a skilled workman guides and controls his intricate machine.

We should never blunder ahead in a mad endeavour to ride rough-shod over obstacles. A child, or even an unreasoning animal, can do that. We should bring into play in any given situation only those powers, thoughts, and ideas that promise to give definite results.

Hence the immense importance of forethought: there is nothing more valuable in the face of difficulty than a calm review of the situation and an endeavour to see all sides of the question.

It is precisely for this that man has been given the power of conscious thought: it is the ability to do this that marks off the intelligent man from his unintelligent colleague.

An hour spent in such a reasoned review of a situation may save many hours when it comes to definite action.

That Tired Feeling!

Everyone who works with his mind or muscle gets tired alter a time. The human machine will only do a certain amount without protesting.

Mental fatigue is, in reality, the same as physical fatigue. So far as we know, the mind is tireless, but it cannot work efficiently in a tired body. Fatigue may be local or general. Manual labour that exercises one particular set of muscles will, in the end, exhaust those muscles. In such a case a change of occupation is as effective as a complete rest.

General fatigue is a more serious matter; a change of occupation in that case would only increase the fatigue.

"That tired feeling" is due to a definite poisoning of the system. The blood gets charged with waste products more quickly than it can carry them away. In such a case nothing is any good but rest to enable the system to clear itself again.

There is no cure for fatigue but rest. Drugs, stimulants, are not only useless but dangerous. It is true that for a short time they may spur one on to greater efforts, but their effect wears off rapidly and leaves the jaded muscles and nerves far more fatigued than they were before.

The easiest way is to prevent the onset of fatigue. Work hard while you are working, and intersperse your work with rest-pauses. And when you rest—if it is only for a few moments— do it thoroughly.

Relax both body and mind. Give the machine a real chance to recover. An hour's hard work followed by five minutes' rest then another hour's work and another five minutes rest, is a good plan.

It is wonderful what a recovery a tired body or mind can make in five minutes. Hard work with well-arranged "rest-pauses" is the way to avoid "that tired feeling."

Think For Yourself!

Earlier in this series I dealt with the importance of habit formation, the importance of associating ideas with ideas, and the value of linking up ideas and impressions.

But the reverse side of this process is an equally important mental function. The human brain, unlike the animal brain, has a tremendous power of analysis.

It is this power of analysis, separating things into their parts, that is the basis of our capacity to reason. If we could not analyse we could not think out the solutions of the problems that confront us.

It often seems to me that the most difficult thing for the average human being to do is to think—not even to think correctly or to think logically, but just to think. We have all got brains; far too few of us bother to use them effectively.

To think effectively means ultimately to think in terms of cause and effect, and to refuse to be led aside by anything except solid fact.

Vague impressions, vague "opinions," hazy ideas are all the marks of the mental sluggard. The thinking man is always busy analysing these vague ideas into their proper proportions.

Equally, a man with real powers of thought can think dispassionately, coldly, and without the prejudice of emotion. If you cannot do this, or cannot argue—which is only thinking aloud—without getting heated, you cannot really think.

Practise this power of cool analysis. Take some political speeches, for instance. Sit down and find out what the speakers really said—as distinct from what they appeared to say. But, bear in mind that no one can think well unless he has a well stored brain.

Knowledge is power all the time. Read widely.

Being Original

Once or twice in these articles I have urged the necessity of striving after originality. Now a correspondent, not unnaturally, asks: "Can a person learn to be original? If so, what is the best method to pursue?"

Originality, inventiveness, creativeness—call it by what name you will—can certainly be acquired to a very large degree. At the same time, some people are undoubtedly born with a greater tendency towards originality than others.

At bottom, originality is simply the capacity to arrange familiar ideas into new relationships. It follows that the first essential is a large stock of ideas. Read, observe, learn from anything and anyone—never cease storing your brain with ideas.

Next, take up some particular study and master it. No one can be original in a general way. Originality must be sought along specific lines—mechanics, medicine, literature, and the like. Choose your line, stick to it, and learn all there is to be known about it.

Thirdly, always be receptive to new ideas. Look for similarities and principles connecting ideas. Often an original thought or an invention rests solely on the discovery of a connecting and underlying principle between well-known facts.

The seeker after originality must learn to think deductively. He must be forever asking "Why?" If Newton had not asked that question when he saw the apple fall to the ground he would never have discovered the law of gravitation.

Learn also to reason by analogy. Notice similarities, and try to apply the principle of one set of facts to the explanation of another set. It is by such means as these that many new inventions are born.

Brains and Bumps

From time to time I am asked whether I believe in phrenology, whether I believe it possible for a phrenologist to read one's character by "telling one's bumps." I disbelieve entirely in [22]phrenology, although I willingly admit that certain phrenologists are good readers of character. But they do not do it by "telling bumps"; they do it because they are keen observers, and keen students of human nature. It is known that certain functions of the brain are localised in certain definite areas of the brain— sight, hearing, touch, motor activity, and so forth. There is no earthly reason, however, why these or any others should show in bumps on the skull. When it is pretended that abstract and complex things like "love of children," "conscientiousness," or "individuality" show as bumps on the skull, the word phrenology becomes synonymous with farce. Nor has the size of the skull (and, therefore, the size of the brain) much to do with the matter. It is the convolutions on the surface of the brain that matter— and these certainly have no outward indication. To be able to say that a firm jaw denotes practical energy, or that soft, delicate hands denote a sensitive and refined character, needs no more than a little observation of men, plus a good memory. And even then the observer will not be right every time! No, the human machine is not nearly such a simple affair as our friends the phrenologists would believe. It needs a great deal more than a certain formation of the bony structure called the skull to explain why one man is an expert mathematician while another is an expert musician. The phrenologist is often quite a good instinctive psychologist; but if he is to be a successful phrenologist he must certainly be a good guesser!

---

[22] Phrenology - The assumption that through external examination of the skull, the individual's behaviour could be understood. Introduced by Franz Gall, a German physician at the end of the 18th century, phrenology was very popular during the first half of the 19th century

Tremendous Trifles

It is not the big things of life that test a man's mental calibre. The real test of mental efficiency is the ability to keep a tight grip on the little things-to organise countless details into a smooth-working and harmonious whole.

If this is done successfully the big thing is achieved almost without effort. One might almost say that it achieves itself, for every big thing has countless little things from which it has been built up.

This is what marks the difference between the trained and the untrained mind.

Lack of system in the day's work, the continual worry because at the crucial moment the required letter cannot be found, work badly planned so that tasks overlap and valuable time is wasted—the accumulated irritation produced by these small things, unimportant in themselves but of tremendous significance in the mass, causes the mental engine to misfire and robs it of its efficiency.

The great men of the world, no matter in what sphere they are found, are all of the same type. They are men who have a perfect passion for detail.

Nothing is too much trouble; nothing is so small as to be unworthy of their personal attention; and they have trained themselves to concentrate their whole attention on the matter in hand, no matter how trivial this may be.

Whatever they do they do with their might. They understand the psychology of the little thing.

The result is that they are spared much of the irritation referred to above. Their brains work with the splendid precision of well-ordered machines. Their whole mental energy, instead of being dissipated along a score of useless side-tracks, is directed down one main channel.

The result is that they "get there." They do the big thing well when it arises because they have learned to do the small thing well.

Dangerous Details

System, organisation, the ability to use the mind as one would use a card-index—all these things can be brought about once the ability to concentrate is acquired. The little things can be either sources of the greatest mental irritation or steps towards the achievement of things really worthwhile. It all depends on whether the mind is going to be used as a crutch or as a dynamo.

If the former, then it doesn't much matter anyway; but if the latter, then it becomes a matter of the first importance to keep the machinery well oiled and running at its highest pitch of efficiency. A tiny speck of dust may upset the smooth running of a delicate machine. The "little things" may be either dust or mental oil. It all depends on the point of view.

This point of view, too, is of some importance. The great men of the world are also those who have vision, who can see beyond the little thing to the big issues involved. They have imagination, and imagination constructively employed will help to rob detail of its irritating tendencies, for it shows the vital necessity of the little things if the big thing is to be achieved in the end.

There is a sinister side to the psychology of the little thing. It is a wonderful obscurer of vision unless the mind has been trained to think logically and clearly. As a "red herring" the little thing stands supreme.

It is perhaps a little superfluous to say it, but for all that it needs to be said, that before one can learn to think logically one must learn to think.

It is imperative that one should acquire the power of thinking logically, the ability to weigh up facts and estimate their true worth, to recognise the essential and distinguish it from the unessential.

Minds and Mobs

It is a curious aspect of man's mental make-up that though the individual may be sane, logical, and responsible, in the mass this same individual becomes illogical and irresponsible.

Listen to any "mob orator" haranguing a crowd: observe any political speaker deliberately "handling" an audience! Neither of them would dare to talk to an individual member of the audience in the same way!

The crowd mind and the mob mentality is a thing as concrete and as analysable as the individual mind, despite the fact that it is composed of nothing but a number of individual minds. Why, then, do otherwise well-balanced minds throw off their logic and their poise when they form units in a crowd?

Largely because it is an instinct to do what everybody else is doing. No one likes to be conspicuous. The fear of offending our fellows, or of being ignored by them, is very deep-seated in us all. Tradition, custom, convention—these are powerful gods we hold in awe, however much we may pretend the contrary.

Such an instinct has its uses and its abuses. It is and should be, the basis of an ordered society, but that is no reason why any of us should act like sheep and follow blindly behind whatever leader offers. Refuse to lose your individuality in a crowd. To recognise the danger is to go a long way to avert it. Keep your logical faculties well in hand and think for yourself all the time.

The mob is merely the equivalent of an unthinking individual, easy prey for the agitator and the crank. You owe it to your self-respect to be as logical an individual in a crowd as by your own fireside.

Tennis Tips

Thousands of my readers will now be busily engaged in playing [23]tennis. Many will be working hard to improve their game. Many more will be starting out to learn how to play.

This article is for them. It is also for all who are trying to establish a habit or increase efficiency. The correct strokes at tennis should become a matter of habit. It is therefore important to set about the task in the right way.

You can, of course, work out the habit for yourself and learn to play better tennis by main strength. If you are wise you will seek advice and tuition from the most expert player you can find.

Efficiency in movement—which sums up tennis—is largely a matter of the elimination of useless movements, and this is where the expert can save you both time and energy. Do not be too proud to take advice from those who know. Both by watching and listening make the most of every good player you meet.

Do not be discouraged if you find progress slow, or even if you find there are times when you seem to be slipping back. No matter what habit we are endeavouring to establish, these periods of apparent stagnation occur, and there is no way of avoiding them.

But as a matter of fact we go on gaining efficiency without realising it. The stagnation is far more apparent than real.

While we are worrying because we do not appear to be making progress, our nervous system is busy assimilating what we have learned, and getting ready for the next upward step. And before we know it this occurs and we find we are "in form" after all, and playing better than ever.

---

[23] Tennis became a very popular pastime within the British middle classes in the 1920's.

The Living Mechanism

Although I have called this series "The Human Machine," and am constantly referring to the mind as a machine, this does not contain the whole truth.

There is one important side of man that marks him out very definitely from the mere machine. Perfect it how you may, you cannot endow a machine with the power of initiative, nor can you give it a sense of personal responsibility.

There is not a single human being who does not believe in these attributes of initiative and responsibility. The whole edifice of the law rests upon the assumption that normal people are responsible for their actions.

If a man wants a job he does not wait patiently until the mechanism of natural forces picks him up and puts him in the job he wants. He gets busy and goes after the job. He is firmly convinced of the value of personal initiative, and believes that activity and energy will get him further than idleness.

We will leave the philosophers to argue whether or not there is such a thing as "free will." The facts of experience point to man's freedom of will just as surely as they demonstrate that there is a law of gravity.

Admittedly, we cannot explain it. But neither can we explain gravity. We have just got to accept facts.

It is certainly a safe rule of life to believe that we are in a position to choose what we will or will not do. It is an essential guide to sane and logical conduct to believe that a man is personally responsible for what he does.

To shelter behind a theory that denies freedom and responsibility is to commit mental suicide. Action brings success, and it is in our own hands to see that the action we pursue is right.

Common Sense

One of the most frequent descriptions we hear applied to people is that they possess a great deal of "common sense."

We all know in a vague way what we mean by "common sense." Let us see what it is in some detail, for it is possible to acquire this admirable character trait. Common sense implies a receptive mind, one able to take in the details of a job that has to be done, and one that refuses to be side-tracked.

It implies keen observation plus the ability to distinguish between what is essential and what is unessential. This ability leads on to the thing that distinguishes the common-sense man from the mere visionary—the capacity to look ahead and make plans based on facts and reasoning from cause to effect.

Observation welded to a good memory can hardly fail to produce a measure of common sense, even by themselves. Will-power, of course, enters largely into the creation of common sense. A trained and powerful will means the ability to persist, to control emotion, and to review impulses and decisions in the light of cold reason.

As important an element as any is the sympathetic interest in his fellows invariably possessed by the man of common sense. In no other way can the wide knowledge of human nature be acquired that enables one to tackle human problems in "a common-sense way."

I have mentioned emotional control; I want to stress it again. Self-control is, in my view, the outstanding mark of the man of common sense. For it is the root of the calmness in an emergency that makes its possessor the envy and admiration of all.

Rose Tints

Roughly speaking, I suppose, we can classify everybody as being either an optimist or a pessimist.

It is human nature to be one or the other. There may be, and probably are, a few isolated minds that refuse to depart a hair's-breadth from the evidence of cold facts, but they are pure thinking-machines devoid of any really human qualities.

Optimism and pessimism both spring from the same cause, however different their characteristics. They arise from a lack of logic.

The pessimist indulges in the time-worn fallacy of assuming that what has already been will continue to be. And he carefully omits any facts that would overthrow his reasoning. The optimist is an equal sinner in this respect. He, too, carefully chooses his facts. "Things always have got better," he says, "therefore they always will get better."

He is, of course, as fallacious in his reasoning as the pessimist; but he is a joyous sinner, and that makes all the difference. For it is largely the optimists who make the world go. They never know when they are beaten. They refuse to be beaten, in fact.

They radiate courage, hope, promise: they infect their fellows with their beliefs, and in the end they literally change the face of the world. For, whereas the optimist looks backward in order to look forward, the pessimist merely looks forward to a life of looking back!

Since we can none of us help influencing our fellows, give me the optimist every time! He may make mistakes, but his motto is always "Upward and Onward!"

Hitch your wagon to a star: it is infinitely better than leaving it stuck in the mud!

Moral Courage

Ever since the deeds of famous men and women were written down for those to read who followed in their footsteps, the unsuspected reserves of moral strength that lie hidden in the human soul have been a source of wonder.

The surgeon can dissect the body and the brain, lay bare the nerves and the tissues, show you just how the machine works and explain its minutest details. But in the last resort there is something that defies his analysis. Behind and beyond the flesh and blood is the mainspring of the whole creation—the soul, the spirit, call it what you will.

We talk glibly of body and mind, but the real puzzle of the human machine lies hidden still. There is a source of power that bids a man stand firm in the face of death itself. Some call it conviction, some conscience; some sneer, others applaud. Those who understand admire in silence.

Each man and woman has a point somewhere beyond which he will not go. Useless to try and explain. It is an individual matter. But to everyone, at some time in his life, this voice of power speaks with irresistible force.

Now this quality of moral courage, when it is sincere and disinterested, is the most valuable force that emanates from the human machine. Moral courage is the lever that moves the world steadily towards better things.

Public opinion frequently derides, one's fellows laugh, mock, and oppress, but the man under a sense of conviction heeds none of these things. He goes on.

Cultivate your moral courage. The world stands badly in need of it.

Mental Revolt

From the point of view of politics and economics, the world just now is a depressing place. Everything seems to be going badly wrong, and nobody seems to know how to "stop the rot."

From the point of view of psychology, the trouble centres both in those who rule and those who are ruled. Mankind has apparently ceased to rule circumstances. One and all we are drifting into the position of willing victims of Fate.

It is all wrong. It is wickedly wrong, since man has the power to dominate circumstances, create his own future, and even create his own present. A nation, no less than an individual, possesses willpower, the ability to learn from experience, and the power to choose whether the world shall be ugly or beautiful.

What is happening to-day is a steady disappearance of the will to work, the courage to tackle and surmount difficulties, and the will to win. From the Government downwards, there is a vague belief that we are helpless in the grip of forces we cannot control.

Such an attitude gathers strength from its own existence. The longer it persists the deeper its roots go. I do not deny that the position is serious. Facts are facts, and they have to be reckoned with; but they must be regarded as a starting-point, not as a conclusion.

Tradition, habit, custom—these are the mental chains that are binding the nation. What is needed is a mental revolution, a complete break with the past, and an approach to our problems with minds freed from preconceptions.

General Intelligence

Several correspondents have written to me to ask what is usually meant by the phrase "general intelligence."

"What," they say, "is the hall-mark of the intelligent man?" Now this is not an easy question to answer; in fact, a good deal of difference of opinion exists as to what constitutes general intelligence, or whether there is such a thing at all.

My own view is that there is certainly a quality of the human machine that we can call general intelligence as distinct from special brilliance in any one direction. My own opinion, too, is that this quality can best be described as a power to adapt oneself with rapidity and accuracy to one's environment.

It is this power of fitting oneself with ease and accuracy into the scheme of things that marks out the man whose intelligence is spread over the whole of his activities. Such a man has other characteristics, of course. He is not impulsive, nor is he haphazard. He thinks before he acts, he weighs up a situation, and makes up his mind with promptitude. And having made up his mind he acts with decision.

I venture to think that general intelligence can be developed by practice. Everybody who is in possession of his normal faculties has a measure of intelligence. The way to develop and expand it is to check and stifle those qualities that make for impulse, obstinacy, faulty judgment, and so on.

I always come back to the same point—think, think hard, think with originality and think logically; but think and keep on thinking.

Made in the USA
Charleston, SC
13 February 2013